A Paxton Year

Eric M. Howe

Introduction

Over the course of a year living in this small New England town of Paxton, Massachusetts, I kept a handwritten daily journal of my observations and reflections of the natural world. This book is the transcription of the journal, with little editing or embroidery.

We live in an age of technological wonder, where it is too easy to artificially experience the world around us. At the push of a button, we can hear the sounds of crickets on a summer evening or see a video of a field of tall fox grass moving in the wind like waves on the ocean. We can use the computer to access the night sky, rotating the heavens on our screen to suit whatever season or time we desire.

Though these things are convenient and certainly incredible, they are a pale substitute for experiencing them firsthand over the course of days and months as the cycle of the seasons unfolds.

This book was written for my family. Through them I learned to enjoy the wonder of this Paxton Year and to rediscover the beauty in the most simple things.

Spring

Awakening

March 21

I planted wildflower seeds indoors today, which is a silly thing to do really, because no matter how prodigious they become, they will be long past transplanting when warm enough temperatures do arrive. I simply needed to do something to counteract this lingering winter, even if it is inconsequential.

I had collected various wildflower seeds last summer and fall, placing them in labeled small glass vials and stored on an old type face shelving on my bedroom wall. It was my intent at the time to plant them in the spring, outdoors when the ground had sufficiently thawed. But impatience has gotten the better of me, so I selected a few seeds from each of the 24 vials and planted them in small soil-filled cells placed within an incubator.

March 22

The birds must be preparing for migration soon. Our juncos are at the ground below, hopping about in a frenzy trying to locate just the right seed to eat. You have to wonder about their efficiency, as they pick up several seeds and cast them away before selecting the one that is for reasons unknown, just right.

Presently there are a dozen in a rough six-foot circle around the feeder base. These are curious little birds, and I imagine them as a jittery meeting of small executioners who are deciding on some fate.

They will leave soon, as they migrate west to the Berkshire hills or north to the White Mountains where they summer in the forest country. Our chick-a-dees will soon do the same, making way for the arrival of our own habitual summer residents of whom we are fortunate to have.

March 23

The Catchfly (Sweet William) seeds germinated today, only two days after I planted them. And they emerged abundantly, as there are over a dozen tiny green seedlings in the cell. I am amazed at this really, that it would spring forth so readily and in such numbers and from what was such a tiny seed – no larger than the period at an end of a sentence, and strikingly coal black. It is a wonder that that such vitality emerges from what seems so opposite.

I read in the paper this morning that scientists are continuing to research the possibility of long-distance space travel, with the potential to colonize Mars or even beyond. Of course, this was the stuff of Buck Rogers years ago, but now it seems that technology has started to catch up with the once fantastical.

Of the rationales for pursuing this, a lesser one highlighted is that through colonization, humans will have a means to continue existing, in the event that we so devalue or deplete Earth's habitable conditions. I am thinking about this as I look into my seedling cell, where a tiny and verdant green forest has sprung up from seemingly nothing.

The scientists also hope that long-distance travel may be feasible to exoplanets that have been identified, particularly those candidates from among the hundreds that have similar characteristics to Earth (distance from a star, certain spectral emissions, etc.) which would then favor habitable life. Perhaps even more, that life already exists in these distant islands in the void of space.

And there's the connection. Out there, somewhere in the seeming inertness of space are assuredly seedlings. Given that humans are apparently destined to ruin those here on Earth, we are compelled to find more elsewhere.

March 24

The chipmunks have begun to emerge from their hibernation. I saw one today sitting on the stone wall by the garden shed just sunning itself near midday. In the summer, our yard and area around the barn has half a dozen of these "seven stripers," as my father used to call them, and we become rather familiar with their various den hole locations. The majority of these are simply emergent holes from the ground, and so I now wonder if the chipmunks have been growing impatient, since the ground still has a half foot of dense snow nearly everywhere.

In a month or so, these little visitors will be scurrying about frenetically, mostly picking up bird seed until nature's provender kicks in with the growth season. Now, I can't help but chuckle to watch this singular newcomer, sitting quietly on the rock, gazing out at the white snow. I imagine that it is trying to determine if it woke too early.

March 25

The forsythia in the kitchen windowsill has small greenish shoots that are emerging from the buds. These are the sepals that cover the developing yellow petals underneath. To pass by and glance, you wouldn't notice a significant change from a week ago, but after a few days in the sunshine of the window, it is undeniable that the flowers are beginning to form.

The same is happening in the soil, still locked beneath the snow that is receding little by little with the warming temperature. Down below, life is beginning to stir and multiply. Worms will soon ascend from the lower soil to begin turning the humus, springtails and mites emerge from eggs, hungry for detritus to feed, and myriads of microorganisms - all part of the vast organic web of life that is within the soil, is capturing energy and cycling matter.

These things take time, and like the clippings on the windowsill, the changes are gradual yet building like a tide toward this thing we call spring.

March 26

A new visitor arrived today at the feeder. It had the look of a yellow finch that was beginning to develop its summer color, but the body shape and markings resembled more a nuthatch.

Sarah took down the bird book and started leafing through it for identification. No mistaking it, we had a Carolina Wren flitting between the feeder and the hanging suet cake. It was slightly larger than our resident house wrens, which should arrive within a month or so to take possession of their established boxes.

The wren stayed for several minutes, unperturbed by the activity of titmice, chick-a-dees, and finches. It suddenly took flight and landed on a lower branch of the big sugar maple near the house, used a small twig to clean its beak (much in the way a knife is sharpened), and then just departed on its way.

March 27

This morning at 5:00 am the full moon dominated the western horizon, only ten degrees or so above the tree line. The early spring full moons are often spectacular, when there is still snow cover on the ground and the air is yet humidity free. With warming temps, it is tolerable even at this hour to be outside to enjoy the pre-dawn splendor of the setting moon. Its light reflected to such a degree off the snow pack, that I could have easily read a book.

This is after all the worm moon, which is particularly ironic this year, as I am quite certain that the normally turning worms are feeling sluggish in the still frozen ground beneath the snow.

Typically, we'd recognize the reawakening of the Earth, in part by the turning of the soil done by the voracious worms within. Or, we would see them by the hundreds strewn about on our paved roads after an early spring deluge has flooded the ground.

No such rains this year. Not yet. Maybe next week. We celebrate the moon all the same.

March 28

A mile and a half north of town is a low land area, where the reservoir from Moore State Park just to the west empties into a wetland basin. It is here in the autumn that I first look to see the colors change in the swamp maples and scrub oak that border the lower ground.

It is also here that I've seen the first signs of skunk cabbage poking up through any remnant ice or snow, greenish yellow shoots protruding upward with a slight unfurling that will become the spreading leaves. I understand the these shoots give off notable heat to aid melting any early spring snow and to hasten their rapid upward growth. This is why you often see just the shoot tips surrounded by ice in certain hollows in the wooded lowlands.

The flower that develops later is the reason for the name, for unlike the perfumes of so many spring and early summer blossoms, the skunk cabbage has a flower which is both unexceptional looking and malodorous, the latter all the better to attract early insect pollinators like flies to the smell of decay.

March 29

March is exiting like the lamb it would appear. After so long in our wanting some substance to the hope that spring will arrive in full measure, today has started with a brilliant sunrise, still air, and temperatures climbing into the 40s at 7:00 am.

I took the dogs for a walk to the lower fields on the northwest corner of Anna Maria just after sunrise. There is a break in the border woods of the college that gives access to a two-track which leads to the farm's roughly 8 acres of land used for vegetables. Now of course, the field remains snow covered, with remnant stalks of corn poking through the snow, small rows of stubble from last year's growth in full.

As we walked the road eastward up the slope toward the upper main field, it was impossible to miss the signs all around of spring's coming. I stopped for a moment, simply to listen and observe those things that only a few weeks ago seemed as though they would never arrive. In the air, birds all around were calling, titmice, cardinals, chick-a-dees, robins, and red-winged blackbirds, each having conversations as if to say aloud, "it is here. It is here."

The sere remnants of last year's golden rod and nested cups of Queen Anne's Lace were beautifully backlit in the sunshine, golden brown against the crystalline snow. Patches of Earth, exposed by drifts and warming sun, showed hints of new green shoots of what will become this year's tall grass.

I closed my eyes and put my face to the sun, listening to the sounds and smelling the Earth-tinged air, warmth of the spring sunshine reminding me that things do begin anew.

March 30

Our front dooryard is enclosed by a small section of split rail fence, which serves as a gate into an alcove that leads to the door to the mudroom. This particular place of the house receives more daily sunshine than any other, and it is the first patch to melt in the spring sunshine. It is also a spot where we've planted several early spring bulbs throughout the years, mostly so that we can look for color when the spring hesitantly arrives.

This morning I noticed two yellow and two purple patches of color amid the mulch we put down last fall. There was also the hint of white.

The day warmed quickly into the upper 40s, with clear skies and a brilliant sunshine upon the ground. Late that afternoon, I made a point of checking on those spots of colors, and sure enough they had emerged into full bloom in the span of only several hours. We had two yellow and 2 purple crocuses and a handful of snowdrops, our first real spring flowers.

March 31

March at an end, and I am glad to bid farewell to this transitional month, which was more like February and less like April.

Still, the changes have come, and if we were able to suddenly compare how things looked and felt at the beginning of the month to how it appears today, we would scarcely believe the progress we've made. This is the way of March, slow changes that really do add up, preparing us for the pace of explosive growth that is soon to happen.

The yellow finches outside our dooryard are showing late March. Just three weeks ago, they were uniformly drab, hardly distinguishable from the house finches that visit the feeder. Today I see them mottled yellow and grey, and I know that each passing day will see less of the grey and more of the brilliant yellow.

Things are coming along, and we feel the spring beginning to accelerate.

April

April 1

My seedlings that I planted two weeks ago are marching along, albeit slowly. Not every wildflower seed I planted germinated, though I suppose one or more could still show signs of life in the days to come. Here is my tally, thus far, given with the number of days to germinate:

Rose of Sharon	9	Butter –n– eggs	?
Sweet William Catchfly	4	New England Aster	5
Balloon Flower	11	Evening Primrose	12
Rose Campion	6	Dock	6
Dandelion	15	Queen Anne's Lace	9
Red Clover	21	Lunaria annua	12
Burdock	17		

The tiny seedlings are still at the cotyledon stage, and each differs in form from the other, somewhat reflective of what the parent will become. They are all little forests of green canopies, and I enjoy lifting the clear plastic lid to smell the Earthy potting soil.

My favorite is the Lunaria, and I am hopeful the seedling will last until I can transplant it.

April 2

The red-winged blackbirds are in full chorus now, particularly just after sunrise. Whereas before we had an isolated male tentatively calling out to no one in particular, now we are assaulted in the morning by a dozen or so that must fly up from the rushes near Asnebumskit.

From here onward for the next two months, our early mornings will be alive with birdsong. These red-winged blackbirds are a favorite, though so many at once are a cacophony.

I've noticed more of the epaulet bars, with some showing both the red and yellow as they proclaim themselves aloud. How the females will distinguish her suitors, when she arrives soon, is a mystery.

April 3

Paxton has several reservoirs, which are protected areas that serve as clean water basins. My favorite is the Kettlebrook reservoirs, which extend just to the north of Route 56 that leaves Paxton, toward Leicester.

I went for a bike ride yesterday past this reservoir, and it's hard not to appreciate the unspoiled view of the waterway and surrounding woods. This time of year it's also hard not to notice the cooler temperatures of the winds that blow across the still icy surface and onto Route 56. It is a pleasure nonetheless to ride the afternoon in the sun dappled exposure on the road, not yet obscured beneath the canopy of trees that soon will be in full leaf.

It is a mixture of sun and shade in rapid succession with northwesterly breezes that carry the chill temperatures of thawing ice. It is April's way of stimulating the senses through light and sound and feel.

April 4

Throughout the years, we've grown familiar with the seasonal patterns of our dooryard bird population. We have a general sense when birds will arrive and when they will depart; some, by virtue of their markings or behavior, we've come to know over multiple years like seasonal tenants.

Every once in a while we are surprised, and today there was a new bird underneath the feeder looking through the cast off sunflower seeds for bits and pieces of detritus. Our bird book indicated it as a fox sparrow, and its markings and behaviors seemed just right.

It searched for food much as does the eastern towhee, kicking its two spindly legs backwards rapidly in what looks like a square dance move, hop back, hop back, search, search. It would repeat this over and again.

The other finches and sparrows didn't seem to pay it much attention, though I do wonder if they marveled or were in aghast of its feeding behavior.

April 5

After a period of no activity, apart from those already on their way, out of nowhere a butter-n-eggs seed germinated, 24 days after I planted it. Admittedly, I had high hopes that these seeds were viable, since I collected them last October from a smallish specimen at a trailhead up island on Martha's Vineyard. I am particularly fond of this snapdragon-looking flower, and I'd like to transplant it if the warmth comes to stay. I envision a hillside full of butter-n-eggs, giving the late summer day a golden and green patchwork, which moves in the wind.

There is such a field here near Paxton, though it is Lupines that cover it in full around mid June. Just down the Holden road, a mile or so after Grove, the road descends sharply and curves toward the reservoir below. On a hill that is the frontage of an old white farmhouse, spread out over perhaps ½ an acre, are wild lupines. When they come to flower in late June, the land is awash in pale to dark purples, set against the greenery and the summer sky above.

April 6

In most years, April is the month in which torrent rains wash the roadways and bring small rivers of effluvial sand and debris down the road. At the end of our driveway, the asphalt is depressed enough that a little backwater of silt invariably collects, leaving a sizable sandbar long after the rains have gone.

The town normally schedules sweeping to occur in late April or early May, and it is our own mechanical rite of passage to hear the big street sweeper coming by the house.

This is an odd year though, and I worry of other consequences in the decisions that the town as supposedly made. There is no sand on the roads this spring, for Paxton elected to forgo using it to treat the snowy roads, instead resorting to frequent application of salt.

The salt, of course, helps melt the roads, and it doesn't accumulate in the way of sand, but it does go somewhere!

April 7

Fred claims to have seen a swallow today flying behind their side barn and circling the fields. We privately joked whether this day should be henceforth marked as the return of the swallow to Paxton, as they say in Capistrano.

They are agile fliers and are not shy about swooping in and among us during the summer when we walk the farm two-track that bisects the field passing near their boxes.

April 8

Early asparagus is nearly ready, and it is evident from the prices in the store how much it has come into season. Just a few weeks ago, a bunch of asparagus cost four times what it does today. Such will be the case with strawberries soon.

It's a strange looking plant, and I remember we had one growing wild in the middle of the backyard when we first bought the house. That first spring I looked out the back porch window and remember seeing the oddest growing thing in the yard – it had the shape of a miniature hemlock tree, all lime green with filamentous branches of tiny endings. I recall it being a couple of feet tall at that point, and it was past the immature stage when the shoots are tender for eating.

Asparagus grows best in sandy soils and should ideally be picked before the main shoot bolts The sandy texture often comes through with store bought plants, because no matter how well you was them, it's nearly impossible to remove all the sand. This is why so often the asparagus will have the gritty feel.

April 9

On Marshall Street, just past Kettlebrook where the road dips down hill and intersects with Hill Road, is a nice patch of wetland on the southeast corner of the road. In a month or so it will be teeming with new plant and animal life, but for now there's not much to show, save for the sere cattail heads and broken clones of rush grass that poke only an inch or so above the water.

I imagine even now that the water can't be more than 40 degrees, and any egg or seed must assuredly wait for favorable conditions. Still, not all is dormant, for the rush grass is now tinged with a deep green, a line no more than 1/8 inch at the base of each clone, with the predominance of dry brown grass sticking up beyond. The cattails too have green at their base, where new growth and photosynthesis are beginning.

April 10

The first honeybees, *Apis meliflora*, visited our crocus blossoms today. It was a clear, still, and relatively warm afternoon, and at some point during the warming day, the first foraging workers must have ventured out to find our pitiful early fare.

A neighbor keeps several bee boxes in the northern corner of the farm field, which is only a few hundred yards as the crow flies, across the road, through the tall spruce line, and over the undulating vegetable field. In the winter, the bees are clustered together inside the hives, ever rotating within a tight ball so that they conserve heat. On calm days in midwinter, when the temperature is so cold outside, I've put my ear to the side of the box and listened to the dull hum of the bees within.

Now I imagine that scouts have been leaving the hives for a couple of weeks, looking desperately for pollen and nectar sources to report back. It's difficult to think that our twenty or so crocuses could cause much excitement, but to look at them now in the afternoon sun loaded with bees going in and out of each one makes you think the pickings are good.

The air is still right now, and I can clearly hear the calls of several birds – some in the spruce line, some in the north woods, and others behind the house near the feeder no doubt. Now joining the chorus are the emergent insects that are beginning to buzz about.

These insects will be the fodder for our new bird migrants that soon will come, our grosbeaks, catbirds, wrens, and orioles. Spring is continuing to arrive.

April 11

It's impossible not to smile at the persistence of the bees as they work the crocus blossoms. In the late afternoon, as the sun begins to dip lower on the horizon, and the flowers start to close up for the day, the bees are still busy trying desperately to poke their way inward. If successful, they nearly disappear within as the blossom shakes about, the insects insistently searching for the nectaries deep within the receptacle.

As they back out of the flower, they are covered in yellow-orange pollen – often so that it necessitates a ritual cleaning. The bees almost perch on the side of the crocus as they use their legs to brush their antennae clean, moving the pollen downward across their body as they wiggle and force it along. Finally, they push as much as they can into the pollen baskets on their hind legs before taking flight again.

April 12

The early morning temperatures were in the upper 40s, and when I opened the side door to listen, seemingly hundreds of spring peepers and wood frogs were in chorus with the dawn birdsong.

I suspect that the vernal pool is teeming with frogs and salamanders now, laying egg masses and calling to mates in what is an assured calendar mark of April.

The Hyla spring peeper has been occasionally sounding for the past several days, as has been the duck-like call of the wood frog. It is as if the early arrivers had been coming to practice in preparation for the main chorus, waiting for a warm night of spring to signal that the calling season has begun.

The tree frog is a tiny little thing, not much bigger than your thumb nail, yet strident enough that its "peep peep" can easily be heard above the forest din. These Hylas are more secretive, and despite their numbers we rarely spot one upon chance. The wood frogs do come to visit in the summer, and we usually see them among the flower gardens, jumping quickly away if startled, their masked face reminiscent of an old-fashioned burglar that has been caught off guard.

And so in all our usual locations, the sounds of peepers and other frogs will welcome us in the pre-dawn and again in the evening hours.

April 13

We had a cool rainy day today, raw feeling really and decidedly less like April and more like early March.

At one point this afternoon, I looked out the front window and counted 14 robins spread out on the front yard, each busy intently on searching for food. It was fascinating to watch, for it was clear that each bird would pause briefly after moving quickly to a new location, cock its head just so to see, and either move on to a new location or stab purposefully at the grass.

I watched a single bird move about this way, and I counted a rate of roughly 1 perceived prey to 4 disregards. Of those times when it did peck at the ground, it seemed to capture some larvae or worm on most occasions. It's amazing really, that its hearing is so acute so as to sense the movement of so small a quarry a half inch or so below the ground.

The day- long rain has flooded the ground, still saturated from the melted snow, and I suspect that the worms and grubs have come to the surface so as not to drown. April rains that deluge so, often cause scores of worms to erupt and make for drier conditions, which is usually the driveway or roadbed. It's no wonder that robins are so plentiful now.

April 14

Some of the spring wildflowers are out in the surrounding woods and wetlands. I went searching this afternoon for May Apples and Marsh Marigolds, but didn't locate a single one.

I did come upon a small patch of Coltsfoot near the outlet of the sewer line road that intersects lower Grove Street almost at the point where it bends to become Pond Street. At first, I thought it was a patch of early dandelion or even hawkweed, with the petals being the same striking yellow, and the shape as similar. The stem was unique though, resembling a braid with small leaflets alternating in whorl from base to flower.

I've read Coltsfoot is a European transplant, now taken to weed, preferring poorer soils that drain slowly. All the same, I'll return in a week or two to collect any seeds for my vials.

April 15

It's been nearly five months since Venus departed as
the morning star, and I am anxious for her to
reappear in evening form. It should be soon, perhaps
within a week or two, we may see her wink briefly
just after sunset, hanging in the twilight horizon of
the western sky.

She will slowly climb, night after night rising higher
in the sky and staying longer after dark, the brightest
beacon in this spring and summer evenings.

Nine months hence and she will revert to our
morning star. The ancients considered her a signal of
fertility, slowly measuring the days from conception
to birth, a shining brilliance in the sky that traverses
back and forth between morning and evening.

April 16

The red maples have gone fully to catkins in
abundance, giving the trees a notably red glow when
seen from a distance. It is particularly evident in the
lower elevations of the hollows near Moore State
Park, which seem to be a week ahead on spring than
our local ecosystem on Grove Street.

The maples will soon pollen, catching up with the
Elm and Juniper that have evidently been distributing

their wares for the past week. I have had a persistent tickle in the back of my throat and a slight scratchiness with all that's floating about.

In a strange way, the landscape has an almost holiday coloring, as the slowly greening lawns and grasses are cast in relief against the glowing red of the maples. It is warming to see the color return to the woodlands and lawns, even if it is so slow in coming. Soon, we will be assaulted with greens and colors in plenty, as life accelerates toward summer growth.

April 17

Morning walks are more inviting than just a couple of weeks ago, and we look forward to the sights and sounds and emotions that are a part of this time. Only yesterday, it seems, did I feel the harshness of late winter's sting, the bite of the air against any exposed skin, the feeble sun, so low in the sky to provide little warmth, or the silence of life still in slumber.

Winter walks are made for introspection, for bundling up to draw our own fires within, as the harsh austerity that surrounds reminds us of our frailties and solitudes.

Spring is our own time to seek renewal, to look once again at the hillside and see the horizon through the still leafless trees. Soon the warmth of the sun will make the vistas hide beneath a canopy of life and leaf anew, and we will be in wonder of the growth and vibrancy. It is a time to look around for yourself and feel the pulse of beginnings.

April 18 In Tucson

The Jasmine is blooming on the vines that cover the adobe house where we are staying. When the sun's rays crest the mountains on the eastern horizon in the morning, they strike a wall resplendent with the vines, and the perfume that is released makes me think of the Egyptian scents that I've only read about.

Small breezes pick up the scent and combine with the smells of mesquite and blooming Palo Verde, and the smell of the desert in the morning is like no other.

April 19 In Tucson

The desert wildflowers are so beautiful, in part because of the harshness in which the flourish. This year I'm told is a good year on account of the rains that came in February and March, encouraging even the most reluctant foliage to display color.

Here are my favorites: The ocotillo are all in bloom and leaf, strange looking stalks with tiny leaves and small fiery red candle clusters on each long arm, looking similar to the flowers of our sumac trees, but more orange in flower than red. The prickly pear pads seem to be in competition among one another to produce the perfect shade of yellow and orange, with some as pink. The flowers on the tops of the pads open quickly at midmorning, when the sun's rays warm the plant. They remain displayed throughout the day, and close again at dusk. Pentsimon reminds me of the Catchfly coloring, striking pink and tiny petals on a light colored and corded stalk. It seems to favor dry washes and trail sides.

The Palo Verde trees are covered in tiny yellow flowers, thousands tucked within its branches, giving the tree a constellation of green and yellow, delicate looking as it moves about in the breeze.

April 20 In Tucson

The sun crested the eastern Rincon Mountains at 6:10 this morning. I was standing on a hill in just a position to see the Tucson Mountains far to the west, the Rincons to the east, and the Catalina Range dominating the north.

The sunrise first shown on the tips of the Tucson range and slowly descended down the slopes, giving the impression of the mountains rising slowly as one to meet the new day. Then, the halo of gold brightened enough on the eastern Rincon in anticipation of the sun's rays cresting the summit and striking where I stood in greeting.

The only sounds that accompanied were the periodic calls of mourning doves traveling among the saguaro forest and the occasional cardinal expressing itself from the top of a mesquite tree.

Quickly did the sun's warmth awaken the desert, and a gentle breeze stirred from the north as if the land were sighing awake.

April 21 In Tucson

Throughout the day a flicker comes to visit, seeking out the red candle blossoms of the ocotillo cactus. It perches near the top and inspects each tiny red flower, bell shaped and in clusters and placed just so that the flicker put its beak in a dozen flowers in a minute's time.

It has the same markings as those which frequent our lawns in Paxton, though its personality is decidedly less shy. Ours will fly low to the ground, stopping almost furtively to search for grubs and insects in the lawn, taking flight at the slightest disturbance. This desert relative pays no mind to my presence below it, seeking its fare and calling below in the way of flickers, a cross between the jay's squawk and the grackle's two-tone alarm.

April 22

The fields across the road went through several changes today. In the morning, row upon row of black lanes progressed from left to right – the plastic covering that shields the plants from weeds and helps retain moisture. This morning, only the sere stalks and remnant leftover of last autumn's crop shown through the orderly holes that occurred at intervals in the black lanes.

Fred began pulling up the plastic in the midmorning, starting at the far end of each row and lifting the edge enough until the wind caught underneath to pull the rest. Long streams of plastic would catch like flags in the wind, shaking off pieces of stuck soil and plant matter. After all was said and done, he packed away the plastic, leaving only the brown of the fallow field, interspersed with small rocks and cast off crops long since decomposed.

Later in the day the tractor was out, spreading lime on the same field. Up and back slowly it went, throwing the white powder in such a way that after it was complete, the field looked as if a light dusting of snow had fallen there.

April 23

As if overnight, the daffodils and grape hyacinths blossomed forth in a profusion of yellow and purple along our walkway and on the edges of the knot garden in front.

We've been watching the daff shoots for over a month, initially seeing them only after having removed the snow drifts enough to locate their small yellow-green blades desperately in search of sunlight and warmth. In the shady spots of the house, the buds are still closed and leaning over from their own weight, though there are indications of the yellow petals that will emerge tucked protectively within the outer sepals.

The hyacinths simply make me smile, each seemingly delicate stalk host to dozens of bell-shaped tiny purple clusters, almost grape-like in both appearance and in odor. Hence the name, of course. The bees seem to prefer them, now that the crocuses and snow drops have run their course.

Spring is giving way to the yellow hues, pinks and purples, as is the norm this time of year. Soon the azaleas will blossom all pink and yellow in various shades. The periwinkle (*Vinca minor*) is also showing evidence of putting forth its small five petal purple blossoms, and I like these particularly, because they look tropical to me, similar to the way in which hibiscus flowers are tucked within the deep greens of its verdant parent plant. Occasionally, the Vinca will produce clusters of white flowers, and I wonder if it is a simple genetic mutant, a variant absent of pigment to the purple norm.

April 24

Someone plowed the field across the road this morning, the same field that had been dusty white from lime these past two days. I heard the "chug chug" of the tractor just after dawn and went out the front door to have a nosy look at what was taking place at the farm so early.

The wind must have been just right, for the exhaust from the diesel tractor drifted by – not noxiously but rather tinting the air in a way that stirred memories of my childhood hauling hay in northern Michigan. There is something distinct in the smell of a running tractor, and the smell of today is exactly the same as that of over 30 years ago, when we kids worked the bales onto the flatbed, pulled behind the Oliver tractor. These are happy memories, of June days in the sun and hard work, where we'd pile tier after tier maybe 9 high onto the flatbed as it bounced along the rolling field. Then off to the mow in the barn, we'd sit high up and stack while the elevator lifted bale after bale, dropping them in succession for us to position.

The tractor pulled the reaching plow behind, turning eight feet or more of soil and mixing the lime underneath. Back and forth he went, slowly creating the newly turned field, which is a dark brown color, moist and laden with small rocks. The fields look clean right now, free of crop and weeds, dust and plastic, and we remark each year that it looks like a field of chocolate waiting for harvest.

April 25

The season's first harvest was gathered today across the road, and we've come to listen for this as a true harbinger of spring readiness.

The tractor moved slowly up and down the field, with front bucket lowered nearly to the ground, and Fred walked just in front, stopping occasionally to bend down and lift the crop into the bucket.

"Bang," followed by another "bang," as each was dropped unceremoniously into the filling maw. These are heavy and make quite the rapport as they collide with one another or the metal bucket sides.

Some call them New England potatoes, and this seems fairly apt, as each year a new crop of rocks of such size and larger are brought to the surface by winter's freeze and thaw forces. It's amazing really, particularly from this Midwesterner's point of view, where our soils tended to be uniformly smooth and I imagine trouble free for the plow and harrow.

Here is just the opposite, and we frequently hear the plow bang against some unseen rock, making the till that much more work. Hence the early harvest, where at least those of observable size can be removed and placed on the field's periphery.

This is after all the region of New England stone walls whose presence pays regard to a time when Massachusetts was more farm land than not. I imagine the work required two hundred years ago to hand cut the timber, clear the stumps, remove the stones by placing them as a wall, and plowing the new land, all by hand or oxen.

We have one such wall that runs from west to east along the periphery at the access road next to the house, down to the lower garden, then lower still until the forest turns, whereupon the wall cuts 90 degrees northward. I'm told it marks what was long ago an actual potato field – not the kind we see being harvested today.

April 26

The full Pink Moon rose just as twilight settled in, and the disk was visible through the still bare trees of the lower woods to the east. These same trees accentuated the commonly held illusion that the moon appears so large on the horizon. It appeared so this night, and indeed the rising disk took on a decidedly pinkish hue as it lifted upward through the distant atmosphere.

The pink name may be on account of the atmospheric conditions that spring affords. Perhaps April has just the right amount of humidity and particles, such as pollen and dust, that the refraction of the sun's rays favor the reds hitting the moon while it is still low in the horizon.

Or perhaps the name is recognition of the pink that frequent the floral hues this time of year, as we enjoy our azaleas and hepatica, and even tulips are possible in the lower valleys of the state.

April 27

There is nothing so fulfilling as the smell of April in the morning after a shower has moistened the land, and the sun has breached the clouds to warm the day.

The scents now are too numerous and rewarding, where only a few weeks ago there was nothing of interest.

The Earth itself is filled with a loamy smell, of green shoots and turning soil, and humus left over from last autumn. The air carriers the scents of elm pollen and daffodil fragrance, and there is the smell of the field now turned and awaiting the plow.

The grass in the yard is greening, and the buds on the viburnum and the lilac are fattening. Soon they will blossom in a perfusion of May.

Even the sidewalks, streets and walkways seem to whisper of life restored, for the ants have emerged, the worms turn out after the shower, the petals of the crocus now past prime lay strewn about, and the infusion of it all with sun and water blends a spring that fills us with life.

April 28

Things are beginning to appear now at an increasing pace, as the weather warms the soil with the sun inching higher in its inclination.

A towhee arrived at the feeder this afternoon, jumping about and backscratching in their way to locate seed. We were doing work on our back deck, which desperately needed sanding and a bit of refinishing for protection, when we first heard the bird's scuffle scuffle in the dried leaves on the berm between the feeder and the access road. Then we saw it take flight to the feeder area, giving a nice view of its markings of orange and black with white pips here and there. These are comical birds to watch search for food, as their back scratch hop reminds me of an old jitterbug dance step, where you jump back and at an angle with two feet, then jump forward at a different angle.

We took the dogs for a walk later in the afternoon, down the hill toward Robinson's Greenhouse, then further on to where lower Grove flattens in an area with wetlands on both sides. When the leaves come out  fully in a few weeks, this portion of the road will be shaded nearly through, and it is a respite from the heat that builds in the summer sun.

Poking up from the deadfall leaves on both sides of the road are fiddleheads, dozens of them maybe five inches high and curled right over in preparation of opening and spreading their broad leaves. These are cinnamon ferns, which tend to prefer the low land areas and moister conditions. I'm told the fiddleheads in their juvenile state are edible, and connoisseurs boil the tender curls to cook the leaves.

Several weeks from now these ferns will have expanded fully, and the surrounding woods will have leafed, creating a darkened and primeval feeling.

April 29

Last evening was the first time in which the chill didn't settle in, and we were able to enjoy 50s well after sunset. It's a decadent feeling to be outside listening to the spring peepers and watching the stars appear one-by-one, while we stand in the driveway with only light clothing upon us.

The sky was as clear as can be, and apart from a thin layer of clouds on the western horizon, the stars twinkled seemingly close at hand. Jupiter was especially bright, perhaps 30 degrees above the west, and Saturn had just risen over the eastern horizon, which was lightly polluted with the Holden lights but not so that it lessened Saturn's shine.

We brought the small telescope up to the town fields across from the college, and I set up the scope to view Saturn. The astronomers indicate that Saturn's inclination just now is tilted so that we have the best view of its polar region, which accentuates its rings as you see them from below and not edge on. Plus, Earth's orbit is closest now to Saturn (though admittedly, the distance isn't that profound); perhaps it's better to express it that Saturn's orbit is closest to Earth.

The scope didn't fail us, and we were rewarded with a spectacular view. Saturn was fairly tiny, but its rings showed majestically.

It is a humbling feeling to view such a giant and know that it is so very far away – so much that the light takes over an hour to reach our eyes.

April 30

April at an end. Late this afternoon, in the warmth of the spring sunshine that we have so desperately craved, I sat in the middle of the front lawn with the dogs, doing nothing more than letting the sun hit my face and listening to the sounds of spring.

The lawn is just beginning to green and lengthen, and the dogs were content to simply sit idly on their sides with tongues lolling out. It is a contentment we could only imagine not too long ago and as much as nature is expressing her desire to "hurry, hurry" toward maturity, I want no more than the pace to slacken now. These are days to be alive, to "rejoice evermore" in the words of New Englander John Adams, who quoted Thessalonians.

The lawn is gathering dandelions now, and they fit nicely among the violets that have been taking hold increasingly each year. I won't need to mow for another few weeks, and that is mostly to even the lawn, yet this first cut also sadly removes the purples and yellows that color the front.

May

May 1

It was light enough to see at 4:50 this morning, and the birdsong was already in full swing, as it will be for the next month and a half. I imagined that they, like me, wanted to cry out "May Day, May Day" at the start of this perfect morning.

I fell in love with May growing up in the Midwest, for it represented the marking point of genuine spring, of school days nearing the end, and of time spent out-of-doors with school mates, playing in the woods by our house. May was still crisp enough that the mosquitoes had yet to flourish, and the sweltering humidity of the summer was still two months away. It was shades of green on every tree, changing daily as new growth moved toward maturity. It was colors and smells to stimulate your senses. It was sweet hay just growing in the fields, still far enough away from maturity which demanded our help in cutting, baling and hauling.

I love May still for all these reasons, and more.

May 2

Across the street they planted corn yesterday in the field that fronts Grove Street and is next to Anna Maria's cross on the hillock of land. To look at the field now doesn't inspire too much, as it is simply a collection of row upon row of plastic bedding that has holes poked through in successions of 12 inches or so.

For our part, we like to consider that the midsummer clock has now been wound in the form of these newly planted seeds, and we will bear witness each day to their progression toward the sweet crop that will result in late July. For now, we are content to simply enjoy the unfolding of our spring, but this planting is an undeniable anticipation of what will be many of our summer meals.

May 3

Wild Strawberries in bloom

The main hill that fronts Anna Maria is covered with tiny white flowers, close to the ground and each no bigger than a dime. These are wild strawberries, and we've noticed that they've been spreading across this hill for several years.

The leaves are also diminutive and in a grouping of 3 leaflets, each notably serrated and also close to the ground. Pull up one of the groupings and inevitably the runners that connect them to its neighbors will follow. Much like the mycorhizzae fungus that inhabits healthy soil, the strawberries on this field are an interconnected mass of reproductive individuals.

Bees and other insects are visiting the flowers now, and with luck in a month we will have miniature red berries throughout the grass on the hill. Most will fall prey to the rabbits, opossum and birds that call this area their habitat, but there will be so many that surely we will have some leftovers to sample. Individually, they don't amount to much, but a handful of a dozen or so tastes somewhat sweet.

May 4

Trillium in bloom.

Several years ago, the college took it upon themselves to raze a long-standing productive vegetable field and adjacent wood that were located next to the campus. They did this to create a parking lot to serve a new dormitory building.

This was a bitter event for the neighbors, who had enjoyed what was a two-track path that skirted the edge of the field alongside the dividing woods. For years, we enjoyed taking the dogs on this track, letting them wander off leash ahead as we simply hiked along observing the successional changes to the field and woods.

There was a spot we knew, just when the edge of the field began and the woodland edging thinned enough to receive more sunlight, that we looked each May to find a small patch of blood-red Trillium, or wake robin, growing set back a few yards into the undergrowth of the woods. The bulldozers destroyed all this, when the land was cleared.

Today I took the dogs down to this area, and we walked along the outlying periphery of the parking lot, as there remains a small buffer of trees perhaps 10 feet wide that separates the college's land from the active farm fields to the north. In nearly this same area, we discovered the trillium again as a small patch of perhaps 10' by 10' growing hidden within deadfall branches that had been rudely piled onto the berm.

I am happy to see these secretive flowers, whose blood-red, three petal blossoms are distinctive, much in the way the spiderwort that flourishes in June has petal colors that are cast in sharp relief against the anthers of golden yellow.

These trillium are a welcome sign of resiliency in my mind.

May 5

Dogtooth Violet (Adder's Tongue) in bloom.

I went down by the wetland area where the road from Paxton to Leicester follows the Kettlebrook reservoir then drops downhill as it parallels the outlet stream. This is one of my favorite sections of the town, mostly because the two-mile stretch passes through protected land, where only the pines on either side of the road and the occasional glimpse of the reservoir command the view.

The skunk cabbage has been in leaf here for nearly two months, and its large foliage lines the stream sides making it easy to distinguish the meander of the river from far away. The water is flowing quickly now, out over the spillway of the reservoir and coursing downhill through the rushes that have seemingly grown overnight. The sound of the water running swiftly and of the periodic breeze across the reservoir that shakes the nearby pines are simply peaceful.

At the bottom, where the road flattens and intersects with Marshall Street, there was a patch of Dogtooth Violet, also known as Adder's Tongue. These are beautiful early May flowers that show their sharply pointed six yellow petals droopingly atop a pedicle flanked by two mottled green leaves. They prefer the moist lowland, though I don't recall seeing them here last year.

The road up Marshall is a steep climb away from the river valley, and the north side of the road, perhaps 100 feet up from the intersection, was a show of red trillium and Early Saxifrage, just beyond the road's edge. Farther still, perhaps a quarter of a mile, the houses begin, and with cultivation goes the decline of these sensitive wildflowers.

May 6

I am thinking of yesterday's Dogtooth find and am torn between the pleasure in discovering them and the realization that such treasures are increasingly rare, I fear.

To read the naturalists of 100 or even 50 years ago, it's painfully true that such wildflowers are vanishing as landscapes are given over to cultivation, management and development. What it must have been like to walk among the roadsides and forests and come upon what these authors so frequently extol as wonders of nature we can now only imagine.

We treat the landscapes as entities to be molded and controlled, with fashioned pathways created and bordered by mulch and plantings. Our spring nature is becoming a composite of predictable series of daffodils, tulips and hyacinths, carefully spaced along synthetic trails amid cultivated and manicured lawns that front roadways in which the remnant salts from last winter await the street sweeper to tidy.

There is simply less wild in the wild, and what threatened bit remains will be gone soon enough. Sadder still is that the artificial created landscapes we experience are increasingly considered as wild nature by those who do not know better.

May 7

The bumblebee has been more frequent around the garden this week. I suppose she has been out of hibernation for several weeks, but the unusually cool temperatures in April probably weren't very encouraging.

It's nearly 70 degrees out today, and I am watching her just now flitting among the periwinkle in the front of the house with apparent distaste, then moving on to the grape hyacinth that divides the driveway from the garden. She is disproportionately large, landing near the top of one hyacinth only to have it bend over with the weight.

The clover is one of her later summer fares, and our own red and white clover has yet to even emerge. In fact, the bumblebee is one of the very few insects that can successfully pollinate the clover, so their relationship is one of mutualism. I read once that Australians imported clover years ago, for it is a ready soil regenerating plant, like the legumes which return nitrogen to the soil. The clover miserably failed, because the Australian biomes lacked bumblebees to help with propagation.

May 8

The maples have nearly leafed out overnight, and our drives around town are notably more canopied in shades of light green. The leaves will continue to grow to full size, and the pigments within will multiply in density, thus darkening to their summer green. They are now emergent younglings, with stems still pliant where the most gentle breeze moves these newcomers to and fro. I imagine that they are simply celebrating being here.

It is worth looking at these maples now. From here on, they will distinguish from one another as sun, rain, blight, and insect take their toll. For now, they look like clones that harken toward the maturity of summer.

Our own vista diminished overnight with their arrival; we can see much less into the woods below, and Asnebumskit is now obscured until autumn. This is no consequence really, as there is plenty to see, smell, and feel just beyond the doorstep.

The birds at the feeder outside the back porch appreciate the building shade and protection. Our big maple is spreading quickly, making the afternoon sun more diffuse in reaching the porch.

The bushes seem to be following suit, and my favorite in the honeysuckle is leafing along just as rapidly. So too our viburnums and choke cherries, both with buds that continue to swell. Our viburnum in front should flower any day now, giving a fragrance that is similar to the sweet honeysuckle of early June. Only the oaks seem slower in coming. They have certainly begun to leaf, but the emergence is less than that of its deciduous relatives. Both our blacks and silvers seem a week or even two behind.

The world is certainly greening quickly, and I swear you can nearly sense the reawakening of photosynthesis all around. The trees are hurrying now to produce as much starch as possible before age and infirmary end another growing season.

Notes:
Wrens arrive at the box.

May 9

There is a wooden fence that runs along the eastern side of Grove Street separating the road from the large field that years ago used to be cultivated farm land. Now it remains as a fallow field, given over to the slow successional changes of seasonal progress.

The sidewalk skirts next to the split rail, and in the morning dawn, seen from a point on the walk, the field is backlit with diffuse golden light made ethereal by the dewy fog that rises from the new growth. From this place, it is possible to imagine Paxton at any point in time, I like to believe, for there are no houses, wires, towers or other indication of human intrusion. There is only the field and forest that borders in the distance.

This morning a mockingbird was perched on one of the split rail posts, and it was singing a dozen different songs as joyously as I have ever heard. I have no idea if it was calling for need or pleasure, but for my part I want to believe that this bird is also just content to simply celebrate spring's full arrival in the field so beautiful.

Notes:
Rose-breasted Grosbeak arrives at feeder

May 10

The mowed fields of Anna Maria are dotted now with bluets, and seen from a distance they look like small white islands amid the yellow green of the close-cropped grass.

Seen up close, the bluets are a delicate clone of small pale blue flowers of four petals with a distinctive yellow center. They grow in clumps of up to 50 or so in arid fields and waste lots. They remind me of forget-me-nots, and each year I mistakenly assign one for the other.

The field right now is awash in these little islands of bluets, and it is particularly beautiful to look across the field from the entrance to Anna Maria up the hill to where the crab apples, standing as sentinels, are also resplendent with their own tiny white flowers. When the midday is clear, it is a sensational contrast of greens and whites, with the blue sky overhead peppered occasionally with its own clumps of spring white clouds.

Notes:
Cowbirds in mating by the feeder
Bluets arrive

May 11

My son and I walked the berm line of the
Asnebumskit Pond dam today on our way to the
remnant path of the far side of the spillway. To the
north of the berm, a bog exists, where the seepage
across the spill empties into a low basin on its way to
the stream that feeds Streeter Pond below. There are
beaver in this bog, and we easily see sapling trees that
bear the marks of teeth, some which have been cut
down entirely leaving only the sharpened remains
behind. This place is home to the red-winged
blackbirds, and our presence sets off a cacophony of
alarm.

As we walked the berm toward the spillway not 100
yards ahead, I noted the blooming of bluets and
strawberries amid the grassy growth and dandelions.
The pond side has new shoots of Phragmites growing
from the sere plants still standing tall from last
autumn. A tiny motion caught my son's eye as we
passed, and he spotted a small turtle hatchling, no
bigger than a quarter, moving just of the berm close to
the water.

I lifted the turtle into my palm, and we watched it
slowly move its head and limbs out from within its
shell. A sudden movement by my son, and the turtle
retreated within, locked protectively away in its little
shell.

We placed it near the reeded water's edge and made
our way to the spillway, hoping to cross the inch or so

of water that flowed over the cement and toward the bog. There was an old foot trail on the far side that skirted the hillside and up into the woods from view. Try as we might, there was no going across, for the flowing water across the algae-covered cement was too slippery for secure purchase, and neither of us felt like splashing overboard into the bog.

May 12.

My favorites arrived sometime this morning, their unmistakable mewing call a give away to their presence around the house. I am listening to them now squawking back and forth to one another in the way only catbirds can.

Like the blue jays, the cat birds seem to embrace mischievous antics, flying in from the berm woods to the suet feeder, and pausing to call in mimicking notes before flitting away to the woods.

They will shift about while perched on a branch, fanning their black tail as in display, while bobbing and calling in their familiar cat way.

Bird books describe them as secretive and shy, yet ours that return year after year seem less so, frequenting the dooryard and flying around the feeders almost in a teasing way.

Notes:
Lilly of valley almost in bloom.
Viburnam in full bloom almost overnight

May 13

The air is resplendent with spring fragrance, and it is almost overwhelming to the senses. A western breeze across the plowed fields brings an earthy smell of waiting soil, passing through the apple tree in front in full bloom and tinted with its unique pungency.

The viburnam blooms are in the thousands, having opened nearly all at once yesterday and each carrying a bit of nectar that smells like a version of honeysuckle, which itself will arrive in a few weeks. These tiny white flowers of the viburnam will linger for a week, before dropping to the ground in a pattern beneath that looks like spring snowfall.

The lily of the valley had bloomed in spots, with bell shaped drops of white emerging from within the unfurled green leaves. Theirs is a scent like no other, and Sarah will bring bunches inside to place on the windowsills.

There is pollen in the air and the smell of both pavement and grass made enhanced by the heavy dew and early fog this morning. All of this is combined with the sense of spring morning, the shifting light through the veiled curtain fog, the sounds of dozens of birds calling to one another, and the tractor in the background making its way down the field to begin transplanting.

Notes:
Oriole returns to feeder

May 14

There was a steady rain last night that must have ended just before dawn for there was a small stream of run off that followed the roadside past our driveway and down the street. The morning sky was clearing, and in the sunrise small drops of water on all the new leaves glistened with thousands of tiny refracted rainbows of color.

Small puddles in the street and in the depressions of our driveway revealed what we knew these past several days had been swirling around us. The pollen had been washed out of the air and now lay in the edges of these small puddles like detritus of yellow washed ashore after a storm. This looks like the yellowing pollen of the maples and even the spruce across the road, though it seems early for the latter to release.

After so many days of needing rain, the Earth will assuredly explode in green growth with this moisture, and the air is tinged with the verdant smell of soil and life.

In the afternoon, we took the dogs for a walk down past Robinson's just to the point where Grove turns into Pond Street. I had wanted to see if the coltsfoot had yet gone to seed for my collection (and it had), plus we wanted to see the water level in the small vernal pool that sits just off the road before the bend (it is a favorite spot to hear the peepers and wood frogs, who call incessantly until you approach near enough in passing, and then they go silent).

On our way back up the hill, just before Robinson's and tucked into the woods on the north side of the road, I spotted a small patch of starflower in bloom, with its delicate seven white petals sitting atop a thread-like stalk. This patch of perhaps a dozen plants, spread out over twenty square feet, sat in the shade of several large pines, in the cool and damp part of the woods that will soon give way to the successional oncoming of the ferns.

Notes:
Starflower in bloom.
Shepherd's Purse in bloom in field.

May 15

The peas have been up for a few days now in the far field across the street, and I went this morning for a walk around the two track that borders one side so that I could see their progress. There are twenty or so undulating rows of perhaps 200 feet each side by side, with small ridges in the middle where the seedlings are spaced one right next to the other. It is pristine looking right now, for each row contains only the pea plants elevated at the top, with the sloping sides almost uniformly of dew-moistened soil and scattered rocks. The only real color, apart from the subtle shades of brown, is the darkened green of the cotyledons and initial leaves, plants no bigger than an inch and showing the first tendrils that distinguish peas so.

Soon the weeds will invade, as weeds do, when the temperatures rise and the seeds that lay waiting in the slopes and valleys of each row remain undisturbed. Left uncultivated, these rows will be laden with mustard, rocket, chickweed and purslane in no time, each competing with one another for space and moisture and resources until chance favors their own expediency to reproduce.

May 16

May is the month of the flower moon, which is appropriate given the seeming explosion of spring blooms that we've had these past two weeks. It is as though we discover a new flower has opened each day, timed just so to receive the increasingly filtered light and to take advantage of differing pollinators that are emerging.

I have been waiting patiently for my favorite to show itself, and today I noticed the unmistakable purple blossoms peeking furtively from within a patch of newly growing grass and poison ivy along South Road as it dips downward toward the lakes of Reservoir Road.

The *Lunaria annua* has returned.

Lunaria, or "Annual Moon" is also known familiarly as the Money Plant, and we used to see it in abundance alongside the roadways of our Kalamazoo farm, as thick as loosestrife to the point that the edges of the road appeared as a purple haze when seen from a distance in spring. There isn't as much Lunaria here in Paxton, though apart from this patch along South Road, it grows abundantly down the Mill Road past Moore State Park, near the old red barn that is used as an antique store.

The Lunaria is a curious plant, and as beautiful as its splash of vibrant purple blossoms are in the spring, it shows a secondary wonder in the fall, when its seed pods ripen. These are shaped as thing green disks, roughly the size of a half dollar, each containing three to five seeds tucked within two outer layers. A plant may have dozens of these pods dangling from various stalks, and in the breeze they wave to and fro like the swaying pattern of the aspen leaves in the wind.

As autumn approaches and the plant dries, the pods lose their color, becoming a translucent yellow that looks like bits of silver dollars attached to the sere plant stalk.

Lunaria is a biannual plant; from seed, it will produce a squat green rosette in the first year, absent of flowers, yet able to overwinter in the strength of the root. In the subsequent spring it grows to the familiar taller plant, resplendent with dozens of purple blossoms. In the autumn, I've collected the dried seed pods and removed the outer coatings and seeds, leaving only the thin translucent inner membrane surrounded by an oval shell. They are beautiful as decorations of an annual moon we keep inside.

Notes:
Robin's Plantain in bloom

May 17

Two rows of lettuce are up nearly two inches on each plant; one row appears to be a regular iceberg, and the other is red leaf, though it may be that the red tinge is only due to their immaturity. Strangely, there is a full tractor width path between where these two rows lie and the start of what will become another plot of some other crop. We've become accustomed enough to recognize that this strip must be unused for some reason, and so curiosity got the better part of me, and I interrupted Fred who was working one of the midfield tomatoes.

Evidently, during transplanting, as they were preparing what would have been the third row of lettuce, Fred indicated that he was driving the tractor slowly down the row in preparation, when he noticed a mother killdeer sitting recalcitrantly on her nest of eggs staring down the tractor in defiance.

Rather than disturb the nest, the decision was made to let the row be fallow, at least for a couple of weeks until the chicks arrive.

These killdeer nest every year in the fields, and their markings, eggs, nests and chicks are almost ideally camouflaged in the soil and rocks of the field. Normally, the only indication of a nearby nest is the squawking of the parent, flying away in a wounded fashion so as to lure away potential trouble. When the chicks do arrive, they appear as small brownish puffballs with spindly legs, walking quickly on fast feet. If they stop, they are nearly impossible to see, hidden so well either by their matched coloring or by the fact that their tiny bodies depart from view when they pause at the bottom of the plow furrows.

I suppose in a week or two, when the eggs hatch, we'll see that fallow row planted.

Notes:
Common cinquefoil in yard
Ruby throated hummingbird appears

May 18

Were we to experience this life for only one day, today is as close to perfect that I can imagine. The frenzied pace of spring growth is just starting to slacken and will settle soon into the productive maturity of what will be summer. For now, the sunshine is as clear as can be, seen through a brilliant blue sky that has yet to take on the sultry humidity of June and especially July. Everything around, seen in the radiance of its light, appears juvenile and full of promise. I am thinking particularly of this after seeing my first mayfly flutter by, pausing briefly to land on my shoulder before continuing onward in a struggle against the gentle spring breeze.

Mayflies remind me of my youth in Michigan, where we would see them erupt by the thousands to spend their singular adult day as a winged insect, searching hurriedly en masse for a mate, flying about over the dock and water before coming to rest and then death on the shore.

Mayflies are frightening to a child, as they look particularly menacing with such long bodies, large wings and split hair tails. They are, in fact, rather harmless, if not a nuisance as they fly indiscriminately about. Mayflies troubled me for another reason, on account of their brief time as an adult.

We learned how the adults emerged from their nymph form and spent a singular day out of the water. It is for this reason that the scientific name of mayflies belongs to the ephemera. Some would emerge on perfect spring days, and we would see them fluttering about in the warm breeze and resting in the warm sunshine. Others would arrive in the cold and rain of a spring storm, destined to know only of their single day as struggle.

I recall being overwhelmed to think of knowing only a single day as life and the cruelty or beauty that such a day might bring. There is profoundness in this, even for a child and maybe particularly so for me, as I know now how filled my summers were with sunshine and carefree days. I know now how fleeting this life can be and that fairness isn't a necessary part of its design.

Notes:
Buttercups appearing near garden backyard.

May 19

The baby bunnies are beginning to show themselves, and we have one that has been curiously and cautiously exploring the side yard near the bird feeder. It can be no more than the size of a closed fist, with richly brown fur, smallish ears laid back flat against its head, and dark eyes, nearly coal black, that watch unblinking for signs of trouble.

We watched it from our sunroom as it tentatively hopped from waning dandelion to new plantain, pausing only to nibble and listen. Often, the rabbits will nip a dandelion at the base of the flower stalk, insert the base into its mouth and slowly suck the flower within, much in the same way that people take in spaghetti strands to be silly. It is comical to watch.

Upon being startled by my opening the door, the little one scampered underneath the medium sized spruce that sits between the dooryard and the berm to the access trail. We walked over to see how close we could get, and the baby stayed deathly still, eyeing us with intent. Had we not followed its movement into the tree, there was nearly no chance of discovering this little one, for its markings camouflaged it perfectly beneath the spruce

May 20

The ants are on the move, both inside the house and out, now that the ground has warmed enough to encourage their emergence. Our sugar ants are particularly troublesome indoors; tiny little things, they seem to enter through window cracks and form small skirmish lines as they forage for any food and water source. We have a small invasion just now as I write this, seated at my desk, with a short trail of tiny invaders coming from somewhere near the sill and progressing close to me by the desk's edge. They don't make it too far beyond, for the cat is decidedly invested in picking them off one by one with her tongue.

Yesterday afternoon, I watched a singular black ant tirelessly work to drag a small fragment of a pretzel across the driveway. It was amazing really, to watch as the ant encountered the piece of food at least five times its size, then slowly drag it across the wide expanse of the pavement. I watched it follow a nearly straight line for twenty feet, I suppose using its antennae to sense the pheromone trail it had left from the nest. When it reached the driveway edge, it navigated the jungle of the lawn, disappearing with its prize into the wild.

Notes:
False Solomon's Zeal in bloom

May 21

I finally took down the old wren house that has been precipitously hanging by a rusty nail in an old oak just within the berm. For the past few years, a wren pair has called this box home, raising often two broods in the summer into fall, always flitting in and out to get food, and trilling incessantly in the manner of the wrens.

I built that box when we first arrived in Paxton, and the years and occupants have taken their toll, with rotting roof and chewed front hole. I recall haphazardly using the first hole saw I could find to create the entry, not really caring about the bird's preference. Even the house was fashioned with no plan to speak of. It was simply a box with a lid, and a trap door underneath so that I could clean out the nest each spring.

Our wrens are just returning this past week or so, as we've heard them trilling and flitting about. I spent a few hours last weekend making a precise wren house, fashioned from plans by the Audubon Society and with a 1.25" entry hole and vented ceilings. I had placed the new box on a stainless steel nail driven in the same location. The old box lay sitting upright on the top of the compost pile.

Today, the new box remains untouched, though I've seen the wrens sitting on the roof of the old one.

May 22

A gentle rain came last evening, coating everything and bringing desperately needed moisture. This morning, in the dewy fog, all the late apple blossom, viburnam and dogwood petals were laden heavily with water, drooping low and tired looking.

With a clearing sun, the wind blew in as the temperatures rose, and I watched the petals seeming to fall in harmony, then blow about on the street in swirls and eddies like snowfall after a light dusting.

It was as if spring were shuddering its final colors, readying for summer's approach, and I for one am simply not ready for its departure. The naturalist Hal Borland wrote that "no winter lasts forever," and I am afraid that such is true with spring.

We still have the sweet smells of our lilacs to remind us of the pleasures of this season, and the growth continues in field and forest with lighter greens giving way to the darker shades of verdant maturity. Our honeysuckles will bloom any day now, with sickly sweet perfume that reminds me of something pleasant from my summer youth.

No spring does last forever, and rhythms of the seasons progress one onto the other, stacking itself into this thing we mark as time.

May 23

The wrens have taught me a lesson in patience in two ways today.

In the mid afternoon, I heard the distinct trilling call over in the area of the new box I put up a few days ago. I had been resigned to rejection, thinking our pair had decided this year to nest in the honeysuckle bush on the edge of the access trail, pathetically only twenty feet from the new house.

One of the pair was flitting about, evidently on inspection, and I sat on the porch for a while to watch its movement. It (she?) would fly up to the box and land on the roof, pause to call in the trilling way, then hop down to the perch in front of the hole, peek in, then enter. She'd stay within for only a few seconds  before emerging to take flight to the nearby woods. This was repeated a dozen times or so, before she seemingly left for good.

A half hour later she had returned with her mate, both entering and inspecting for a few minutes, then starting foraging trips to the woods for small sticks. I was smugly proud that my box was deemed acceptable.

I was, admittedly, concerned about the intelligence of its new occupants, as each would return with nesting sticks that were rather long and sinuous, clearly intended for base material in the bottom of the box before the upper layers of grass and fluff would be added. The birds would hold the sticks cross-wise in their beaks and try to enter the hole, failing of course as the sticks became caught (illustrating perfectly the adage of long pegs not fitting into round holes).

They would poke and prod, often dropping the stick to the ground, causing them to fly to the woods in search of another. Patience however did win the day, as the birds seemed to figure out the trick of tilting their heads to encourage the sticks to go end first, and I am happy to report that they have been busy ever since building and singing.

May 24

Several roadsides on the outskirts of town, particularly those whose shoulders remain uncultivated, have wild geranium in bloom just now. My favorite is the upslope of Nanigian Road, just before it intersects Barclay Road (which becomes Rockland as you head toward Treasure Valley).

Here, amidst the green of new foliage, peeks through the showy pink flowers, each with five petals, rounded at the edge. There are fewer shades of pink to found in general now, as spring gives way to approaching June, where irises, lilies, and other early summer flowers ready themselves in purples, reds, oranges and yellows.

The stretch of road is far enough from the center of town that it is easy to see the agricultural history of Paxton; just at the top of the hill is a fallow barn, with hints of foundation to some structure, likely a dairy barn across the road.

To the left, down Barclay is a going farm with dairy cattle, I think. I enjoy passing here on the road to see the aging farm house, bleached white with blackened wooden shutters and a small porch in front. They keep a sign across the road that advertises hay bales for sale, $2.25 or thereabouts, and in the early summer the smell of mown and baled hay is everywhere in the air.

In a week or two, the geraniums will lose their petals, giving way to the developing seed pod that grows in an usual shape and gives the flower its common name, spotted crane's bill.

May 25

We've finally received a stretch of good transplanting weather, and we'll take it even if it is overdue. Rain has been steady since last evening, and the forecast shows cool and damp for the next couple of days.

In anticipation, they were busy across the road at the farm yesterday. Dozens of flats, with thousands of seedlings of differing vegetables, were brought forth from the greenhouse and placed on the driveway in front of the store, ready in queue for the transplanter and the field. It was non stop afterward, and I watched the tractor slowly making its way down rows across the street, with Fred and Louise seated low in the surrey chairs behind, picking plants out of the cells and placing them one-by-one into the holes just poked and watered by the transplanter wheel, as it slowly progressed down the row of plastic.

I took the hint to follow suit, taking my single flat of seedlings out of the cold frame and planting the three raised beds in the lower garden. This year will be cukes, peppers, lettuce, tomatoes, and squash, provided that the fates work in our favor and against the chipmunks, rabbits, crows and slugs, which have one or more given us headaches in the past.

This morning in the drizzle I walked between several rows of peppers and eggplants across the street, admittedly nosy in my admiration of yesterday's work. It's a pleasant sight to look down a row that is 300 feet long and see plant after plant of small seedling clones, each a vibrant green and yet blemish free from disease or pest, cast in relief against the black plastic and weed-free soil between rows. It is idyllic and fresh to see the seedlings at this stage.

May 26

The mints in the front knot garden have gone to flower, delicate and small their blossoms of pale purple and blue. We have several varieties of mint both in the garden and growing wild in the periphery of the lawn – cat mint, spearmint, lemon balm, and wild bergamot (or menarda). The latter has yet to even consider flowering, but in late June we should see its buds of soon-to-be fluffy blossoms of purples and reds. These are the bee balms or Oswego teas, and our visiting honeybees will frequent their area when the flowers arrive. The brilliant red of the bee balm also attracts our hummer, who can't seem to stay away from the red splash but evidently isn't overly satisfied, for he moves quickly onward each time.

The mints are a distinctively summer scent, and I enjoy tearing a leaf and rubbing it between my fingers. This is doubly so for the lemon balm, as it has a pleasant smell, which I wonder if discourages mosquitoes, much in the manner of eucalyptus.

Mints remind me of the shoreline vegetation on the lake in northern Michigan, where we would travel down to the far bay and beach our boats on the sandy shore. This area of the lake is kept pristine from human intrusion for several miles as has always been, and the shoreline today is the same as it was in my boyhood explorations. We'd walk the beach, dotted with reed grass and mint, where emergent toads by the hundreds would scurry away when approached.

I think of these memories nearly every time I tear a
piece of mint to rub.

Notes:
Ruby-throated hummingbird returned to feeder.

May 27

The skies cleared late this afternoon following this
bitter late spring nor'easter which brought rain and
even a few flakes of snow so close to June. Looking
ahead, the barometer is on the rise, and high pressure
will bring a return to normalcy, a fact that is
confirmed by the weatherman who forecasts upper
70s within a couple of days. Had this been midwinter,
the result of this storm would have been feet of snow.

Just after sunset on the western horizon, an absent
friend has returned and is now partnered. Venus and
Jupiter are within a half of degree of one another,
making a bright pairing even in the twilight sky.
Astronomical charts also indicate that Mercury is
quite close, but the skies are simply too bright to
permit a viewing of this fickle planet.

Venus will be rising now, steadily each night,
assuming her position as the evening star as she
swings in her orbit catching up to our own and
getting closer with each passing day.

The twilights are now noticeably longer, and so
distinct from winter. These are the evenings where

the grayish veil persists long after the sun dips below the horizon and also the light that ushers in the daybreak and birdsong at 4:30 in the morning. Astronomers explain it as the inclination of our axis, where the directness of the rays persists after sunset. We simply enjoy it as a softening of the evening, a chance to breathe after a working day or a time to ease awake in the morning before the chores.

Twilight and Venus in the evening sky feels like summer is slowly approaching.

May 28

Increasingly on the side streets, where the shoulder borders any woodland or wetland area, the Chinese Knotweed has become established. It was diminutive only a week ago, but now it is flourishing, growing at what I'd guess is an inch or two a day, spreading its bamboo-like stalks in a clone form and even readying its buds.

I purchased a small pamphlet on Massachusetts's invasive plants, written in 1999, and browsed through the twenty pages or so to see how many we have here in Paxton. Unfortunately, we have nearly all, and several species that the authors list as potential troublemakers in 1999 are ubiquitous menaces here now.

Several weeks ago, I wrote about the reduction of our wild native plants, particularly wildflowers, and in no small way these invasives are contributing. They establish and grow and outcompete, robbing the natives of space and light and nutrients until only the invasive itself seems to exist as a monoculture.

As I write this, the garlic mustard has flowered and gone to seed, its many white petals falling away by the roadsides only to disperse thousands more offspring. The loosestrife is growing on the sedge zones of Asnebumskit and the lower marshes along Route 122. In a month or so, it will reveal its beautiful flower heads, each so fecundate that it is nearly impossible to prevent. We have our bittersweet everywhere, wreaking havoc on our bushes and trees, choking them as it climbs ever higher. There is the burning bush all over yards and borderlands. And the multiflora rose has taken hold, bearing sharply thorned stalks that invade like briar, making it difficult to remove.

May 29

I noticed that I left something off my list of invasives yesterday. I did so unintentionally, though I can't deny that it is one of my favorite shrubs this time of year. As I sit here now in the late afternoon sun, the smell of honeysuckle is carried all around, a slightly sweet fragrance that would seem more fitting to accompany a sultry midsummer night than a waning spring day.

The bushes seem to thrive here, and I know we should fight them by pulling and burning – after all they do crowd out the understory and shade-tolerant greens. But those small white flowers by the hundreds perfume the air, much like Jasmine we experienced in Tucson.

It is true too. Pluck a honeysuckle flower when it is ripe, pull of the petals and sepals till only the receptacle remains. Begin by pinching below the receptacle on the stalk, and roll your fingers so that you slowly squeeze, and the tiny nectaries within will reward you with a single small drop of clear nectar that does, indeed, taste like honey water.

May 30

Last night the temperature didn't go below 60, and we were witness to a storm of lightning and wind near midnight, leaving the dawn leaf strewn and sultry. May, it appears, is ending less like spring and more like summer, and it is strange to think it nearly snowed only a few days ago.

The first crickets were chirping last evening as if to welcome the transition to June. Their strident calls are still tentative trials of new legs and rasping fiddles that will become more proficient over the next several weeks. I imagine that the grasshoppers have molted twice since they emerged; we saw a couple near the front garden several weeks ago that were tiny versions of the adult, surely the first instar that will grow slowly to become the big jumpers and flyers of our midsummer.

Fred was transplanting leeks across the road, placing seedlings one-by-one into punched holes in the row of white plastic. The white is stark against the predominant browns and greens, but it is a precautionary concession to the coming heat of the next several days; little leeks may burn in hot soil below the traditional black.

I walked the fallow row toward home after checking the transplanting progress and to see how the parent killdeer were faring. Despite being told by Fred the approximate location of the nest (near the end of the adjacent row of scallions), I almost stumbled right upon the small pile of rocks, pea sized, that were just in the open.

No chicks as of yet, but both parents made a fuss at my approach, placing their wings outward in a bow, calling and stumbling along the ground as if to encourage me away. I caught a glimpse of only a single egg, camouflaged like a rock, amidst the nest.

Notes:
Milkweed flower buds appearing.

May 31

May at an end, and I confess that I am always sad to see it go. June will bring its own wonders, and we will assuredly enjoy its warmth and light. But May has always filled me with renewal of spirit to see so many things reawaken fully in the rush to grow.

The dandelions that remain are mostly dressed in puffy white seeds, ripe for picking by children of all ages to blow and watch as thousands of white parachutes fall gracefully amid the current of air. So many thousands of seeds, and yet some will, despite improbability, survive to create next year's plant.

These dandelions are a miracle really. One day they remain our familiar yellow form, a myriad of compound petals with seemingly as many tiny stamens within. Then, overnight it seems that they transform into the blowies, as we call them, no less a miracle in process as it is to behold.

It is nature's exemplar of design, a perfection of engineering that William Paley might consider as evidence of an omnipotent creator. Its dispersal is a wonder, and its fecundity astonishing; I once kept seeds for three years, small parachutes with their treasure, tucked in a jar. Nearly all germinated upon planting.

June

June 1

It was hot enough today to go barefoot just about everywhere, and our soles having been so long shod for the last several months felt strangely liberated in the dewy grass and hot roadbed.

Our feet are as tender as this meteorological summer which is casting off the cloak of a growing spring and settling into the business of production. Walking around was a tentative affair today, and more than a few times did I wince at some stick in the yard or hot spot of the pavement, gingerly repositioning my feet that need more time to adjust.

As children, my sister and I would arrive to the woods of northern Michigan after school let out, and we would forego shoes from the outset, though gingerly stepping on pine needle bedded pathways laden with acorns and leaves, roots and shells – paths that were our childhood highways from the cottage to our adventures near the shore or in the woods. We were tenderfeet in many ways those early June days of our childhood, carefree and full of promise much in the way this month begins.

Our feet would toughen, and the ginger steps and wincing movements became less and less as we accustomed to living in summer.

Notes:
Chickweed blooming in yard.
Wild columbine blooming.

June 2

Walk the top of Davis Hill Road, on the knoll where
the farm sits adjacent to the cresting field of sweet
grass that is now waist high. In the morning sun, the
gentle breeze causes waves in the grass just like the
ocean, and you can see the undulations and shifts of
the wind across the field.

Summer flowers are arriving in earnest now. The heat
of the past few days has hastened their coming I
suspect. Just here, tucked at the roadside between
thinning tufts of sweet grass are bladder campion in
bloom. There is also cow vetch and even red clover,
both healthy looking, and I am surprised to see it this
far along so early in June. A little further on, where
the road descends sharply toward Route 122, daisies
are out, white splashes bunched together with vibrant
centers.

Notes:
Sweet William Catchfly blooming.

June 3

The warm spell of last week has accelerated the
arrival of the mosquitoes. We seem to have two
versions just now, small ones that don't sting when
they bite and large ones that most certainly do. The
former tend to congregate in the periphery of the
yard, near the wood's edge and low to the ground.
It's only after you've glanced down at your exposed

ankles that you notice them and then too late. And my, do these little ones cause an itchy reaction.

The big ones are roamers, and they will follow persistently wherever you go. I just walked down to the lower garden from the porch, crossing over 100 feet of lawn, all the while waving my hands and slapping at my exposed skin. From a distance, I imagine I looked like a man out of his mind, walking and slapping (and cursing).

By coincidence and design, the dragonflies are also appearing. Each afternoon I've seen more of them hovering in the air ten feet or so high up, darting about looking for food.

Notes:
Spiderwort in full bloom.
King Devil beginning.

June 4

It really is worth observing the dragonflies, either in flight or at rest. My childhood summers in Michigan were filled with both dragonflies and damselflies on account of the lake and surrounding wetland. We had no shortage of insect hatches, and the big dragonflies seemed always on the move or resting on the dock in the summer sunshine.

I don't recall being afraid of the big ones, since we were surrounded by them since childhood, but I suppose the first few encounters were a little terrifying; they are intimidating looking and will remain relatively still until you just approach. We learned a technique for bringing our hand in slowly, with finger extended, putting it gingerly underneath the monster's eyes until it reacted by climbing onto our finger. These were our own pet dragonflies that would stay so long as we didn't move suddenly.

They would be up to 5" long from menacing head to reticulated tail, green and black stripped, with small yellowish spots on their thorax. Their eyes were iridescent facets of green, bulbous and sinister, and they would cock their heads quickly as if regarding how best to eat our finger.

On occasion, we'd discover a newly created adult, just emerged from the nymph after undergoing a metamorphosis to develop its mature form. We'd see them hanging, tail downward, wings yet extended and deflated looking, waiting for the blood to flow in its capillary structure to both firm and harden its final form. Dry for half an hour, then off it would go. Another summer miracle.

The damsel flies seemed more personable somehow, yet untamable to us boys, and we'd have to content ourselves in just watching them, often in looped pairs, flying about. It wasn't until I was older that I learned about the meaning of the looped pair business.

June 5

Transit of Venus

Exactly one year ago this very day we witnessed a
miracle – two really, if the manner of its appearance
could also be counted.

We had known for months (years actually) that the
rarity of Venus passing directly between the sun and
the Earth was to occur on this very day, and viewable
for much of the event in our location. These transits of
Venus are celestial rarities, happening in pairs
separated by eleven years, and then not again for over
100 years. The transit of eleven years ago wasn't
visible from North America, so we had just this one
chance to view the transit. After this, very few people,
if any, would be still living to witness the next.

Halley predicted transits of Venus in the early 1700s,
and he instructed future scientists (known then as
natural philosophers) of the 18th century to mount
expeditions to the far corners of the globe so that the
transit could be viewed from differing locations. With
variant timing of the entry and exit of Venus across
the sun's disk on account of different vantage points,
Halley claimed that parallax could be used to
calculate the relative distance of the planets in the
solar system. Halley knew then that he'd never live to
see his instructions carried out, as the pairings
weren't until 1769 and 1780, well after his own death.

It is astonishing and inspirational to read accounts of
the voyages and hardships undertaken during both

these early transits, with years spent in preparation to capture the few precious hours in which Venus ingresses, transits, then egresses the sun's disk. So many factors could conspire to thwart the effort.

We had been waiting for weeks, knowing just like the explorers of 200 years ago when to expect the transit's beginning. With luck, we'd have a few hours of viewing, before the evening sun would set below the horizon, preventing our egress view.

Four days prior an unusual nor'easter arrived, with cold, wind-driven rain that was forecasted for days. It was as cloudy as a bleak November stretch, and the morning of the transit saw a misty rain. At 4:00 pm, the clouds showed signs of breaking, with individual cloud shapes taking form among the leaden sky. At 5:00 there were small patches of blue, and we quickly ferried our telescope up to the farm parking lot to set up and wait.

Ten minutes out, the clouds parted, and the sun shone brilliantly for the first time in days. I held a white sheet of paper in front of the eye piece, set back far enough so that the image of the sun from pointing the telescope in its direction was cast as a dinner-plate sized projection, complete with sunspots shown clearly on the paper.

With our friends as witness, we watched. "There!" someone called out, and the first bubble of Venus made its push into the bright disk, as a tiny dark circle slowly traversing across.

We watched in silent wonder for fifteen minutes, knowing that millions of miles away Venus was directly in line between us and the sun, moving inexorably in its orbit like a celestial machine, predicted for this very day over 200 years ago.

The clouds closed back upon us, and the sun shone no more that day. It was indeed a miracle.

Notes:
Yarrow in bloom
Birdsfoot Trefoil in bloom.

June 6

I came upon a small snapping turtle this afternoon making its way in earnest across Grove Street, having just exited the Anna Maria field and headed in what I can only assume was toward the wetland  on the pond. Why it had come from the fields is a mystery, but it was making this journey in a seeming bee line; I watched it going slowly across the road, until concern impelled me to give some assistance.

This snapper was approximately 6″ in diameter, coal black, and full of energy. Unlike its painted cousin, which will go docile within its shell upon being handled, the snapper was all fight, wriggling in defiance and trying to use its clawed legs to dislodge my grip. It was successful, as my hold was tenuous to begin, seeing that snappers have the reputation of a nasty bite, and I dropped the little thing back onto the road.

 Wouldn't you know, it pulled its head in slightly, splayed out its back legs and reared up and down somewhat rhythmically, seeming to take in air with each lift and expel it forcefully on the down. This made a slight hissing sound which only reinforced my decision to leave well enough alone.

After a few moments, it resumed its beeline, finally making the tall grass on the opposite side of the road, headed toward more peaceful locations.

Notes:
Blue-eyed grass in bloom
Deadly nightshade in bloom

June 7

The plowing work has mostly finished across the street, with rows having been prepared and seeding accomplished in roughly half. The remaining await the transplants, which presently occupy the driveway in front of the store, having been moved out from the greenhouse. Here there are thousands of peppers and eggplant, sitting in flats, each plant six inches or so tall and nicely green, miniature clones of one another that sit soaking in the sun.

The tractors still run, though the yolks are now affixed to the cultivators, and the runs proceed up and down the rows of growing corn, still 10" high, cutting the roots of the wild mustard, ragweed, purslane, and shepherd's purse which have taken residence in the valleys between the corn.

The cover crop of rye and vetch is healthy in the fallow field that sits below the knoll. Purple flower clusters speckle within the rye, which themselves sheen a silver teal in the afternoon sun. I suspect this field will be plowed under soon, returning the carbon and nitrogen to the soil and thus adding to its fertility for future plantings.

June 8

A summery high pressure moved in after such a period of languishing humidity and doldrums. It must have been notably still these past several days, as a gust that came this morning, seeming to herald the arrival of the change in weather, shook the spruce line across the road so that a mass of pollen was released.

It was as if a living cloud had been instantly created, and we watched in wonder as it moved quickly across the road and toward the house, shifting and mixing visibly in the current of air like a yellowy swarm of insects or a large flock of birds when seen at a great distance.

In seconds, it was upon us, passing through and over, hitting the house and lifting up and over the roof, leaving in its wake a thin coating of powder-yellow pollen on everything, including us, who could only stand helplessly assaulted by the spruce's output.

Notes:
Purple/pink phlox beginning to bloom.

June 9

There is an old trail, long fallow, that runs behind the Klingele Fields, beginning at the top of the hill within the woods on the southern end and extending through the ridge. Several years ago, this path was more apparent, but the ice storm of 2010 brought down so many limbs that it is now barely recognizable and most certainly untraveled.

One hundred feet into the woods are the remnants of a camp house that stood here decades ago, belonging I'm told to one of the David sons who worked and hunted these lands long before their development. The trail passes beside the dilapidated structure, then descends somewhat precipitously on the slop that leads to Asnebumskit Pond.

Where the trail begins, I discovered a small patch of wild geranium amid the more plentiful yarrow that is now coming into its own. Also there was a pleasant surprise of blue-eyed grass – something I've not seen before, apart from photos in books. It reminded me of lake reed grass or sedge, with flat blades that rise in a clone, each with a cluster of flowers just beneath its top. These blue-eyed plants have groups of small lavender flowers, which catch the passing breeze and cause the whole clone to sway.

Notes:
Wild rose in bloom
Lavender in bloom

June 10

A tropical storm came through last night, bringing torrential rains that lasted for hours, leaving the yard and driveway littered with leaf fall and puddles to greet the morning light. The weatherman proclaimed we received nearly four inches in our area, and I do not doubt this after such a deluge.

Like all fast storms that race up the coast, this moved onward by early morning, leaving a breaking sky in its wake - low-level clouds that swiftly moved by, where upper cirrus and blue sky appeared in pockets in between. By eleven o'clock, the sky took on a summer look, with brilliant blue and white puffs of cumulus clouds floating in shapes overhead.

Across the road, in low spots between the rows, puddles of water sat awaiting the already saturated ground to discharge, and the hatchling killdeer chicks used the plastic rows as islands for travel, looking like little cotton balls moving swiftly up the black lining, dodging the growing lettuce which is now the size of dinner plates.

June 11

The north road on Wachusett Mountain begins as an access trail, two-track with tufts of poverty grass and stone bedding in between. It starts at the base of the ski buildings and winds upward criss crossing the cleared ski slopes and rising steadily counter-clockwise up the mountain, through several patches of what appear to be old growth forest.

After approximately 2 miles, the road has gained nearly 1000 feet of elevation, and the landscape is transformed to a state of vegetation that we experienced two to three weeks ago. In short, we felt as if we'd stepped back in time to late spring, with bluets in the roadside ditch, hyacinths doting the rocks, and patches of violets in the wetland glades seen from the path.

The air was noticeably cooler here and cleaner feeling somehow, and we had the road to ourselves as we ascended to the point where it exits onto the paved mountain road. Here, at the gate that prevents cars from gaining access from the mountain road, we skirted the iron crossing by going round near the woods. Just there in the shady wetland of the woods stood a singular and perfect lady slipper, back lit by a shaft of sun that found entry through a hole in the canopy overhead.

Notes:
Orange hawkweed in bloom.

June 12

The roads were damp this morning from an overnight
shower, brought in from another tropical front out of
the south. Daybreak saw high humidity from the
outset, leaving the saturated ground and leaf cover
heavy with moisture. It had a heavy feel that hinted at
midsummer yet to arrive.

The moisture somehow brought out the odor of the
wild roses, having come to bloom within the past few
days, and in some places lining the roadside edges
with their white blossoms. They resembled
strawberry flowers, only larger and clustered
together, and their fragrance just now is intoxicating.

South road has roses on both sides, particularly for
the first few hundred yards as it leaves the Holden
road, where there are no houses to interfere. There is
just the tunneled canopy of green, maples and oaks,
ash and hickory, and the roadside ditch is filled with
wild rose, so much so that it is a contrast of perfume
when traveling by.

The moisture has brought forth another seasonal
migrant; the spotted red newts are evidently on the
move. These delicate little creatures will be traveling
to and from wetland locations, just now in the eft
stage, which is distinguished by their almost

luminescent orange body with tiny reddish spots. They are tiny things, no bigger than an inch or two, and they move with the speed and purpose akin to the sloth – slow and deliberate, placing tiny feet one after the other in slow progression.

They are easy to spot now, when contrasted against the dark wet pavement.

June 13

Each time I go out to the barn, within ten feet of passing near the burning bush that sits on the front corner, the mother robin emerges from within and flies away low and straight toward the berm woods.

I feel guilty about disturbing her so, but one does have to wonder about the sense robins possess when planning the logistics of nest building. Our robin pair that has been coming for ten years, albeit likely a couple of  generations of the birds, inevitably decides to build their nest in either the viburnum bush in the front of the house or the burning bush by the barn. This, despite the fact that these two locations are heavily trafficked by us.

I notice throughout town a similar pattern. The robins seem to prefer human activity, yet when it comes to time sit on the nest, any interruption is met with protesting cries and taking flight in the manner of these birds.

I decided to peek yesterday, after the mother had taken to the woods. There within the bush, the nest contained two babies, nearly at fledgling stage I'd guess by the look of them. They regarded me silently with beady black eyes and mouths slightly open, feathers still tufted with downy-like fur.

I stayed long enough to whisper to them that should they decide to return here next year, not to build their nest so close to the barn or house; they would be welcome nonetheless.

Notes:
Daisy fleabane blooming

June 14

The orange hawkweed, close cousin to the king devil, is popping up now in the open fields and roadsides. There are still plenty of the yellow king devils to be found, easy to spot with their clustered dandelion-like flowers atop tall, hairy stems. This year was a mast year for king devils, if such a word is appropriate for wildflowers; the town seems to have them everywhere these past couple of weeks.

The orange hawkweed has been slower to arrive, despite its close association in form and habitat. It is the prettier of the two, with sunset orange clusters that open with daybreak and display their contrast well against the greens of the open fields. This flower goes by the name Devil's Paintbrush or Indian Paintbrush in the vernacular.

When seeking a plant suitable to study hybridization, Gregor Mendel was encouraged to consider hawkweeds as his model. Though pretty, they don't exhibit the dichotomous characters as do the peas, and had Mendel chosen the Devil's Paintbrush instead, his mathematical observations may have been delayed for another to discern.

June 15

June is the month of the strawberry moon, and this is aptly named just now. Look closely at the roadsides and open fields throughout town, where only a few weeks ago the white blossoms of the wild strawberry have given way to splashes here and there of tiny red fruit.

There is a large cluster at the top of Streeter Road, tucked secretly within the tall grass and bindweed that have outpaced the strawberry since flowering. These berries are unusually large for wilds, and I am happy to report that they are surprisingly sweet.

More often the fare are smallish, and it takes perseverance to pick enough to satisfy any hunger pains. This really isn't the point though – it is enough to be out in the field walking in the June sunshine which has contributed greatly to this early summer reward.

Be quick about this, for there is competition to be had, as the birds will undoubtedly descend; they need it more than we, I suppose.

There will be cultivated berries galore in the store now, and I am reminded that the farm opens soon, made plain by the sign out front which reads "Opening around June 22 with strawberries and early vegetables."

Notes:
Milkweed in bloom

June 16

Notice the lawns in town about this time to see the successional change from spring to summer. This doesn't apply to the subset of manicured and treated lawns that some invest, where the created monoculture of blue grass or fescue is unnaturally emerald green and weed free. I frown upon these ornaments that display perfection at the hidden cost of herbicides and insecticides. These are not healthy lawns as some might proclaim, any more than to suggest an artificial Christmas Tree is natural looking.

The healthy lawns have crabgrass just starting to emerge, its pale yellow blades filling in the thin spots having germinated with warmer night temperatures. There is also still Cinquefoil mixed in, though waning since it first appeared in May, and Yellow Wood Sorrel remains, brought back to vigor from recent rains.

Plantains have spread their broad leaves low to the ground, avoiding the mower in anticipation of sending its flower stalk skyward. Dandelions are all but gone, as are the single-bladed Canada Mayflower, having gone to seed I notice in the periphery of the yard.

June 17

Surprises do appear, even in your backyard.

On the side of the barn in back, the one that faces the north where shade predominates most of the day, the ferns have taken hold and are fairly well along. I pass by this area twice a day on my way from the house down to the garden and back again, and aside from the ferns and the singular mustard plant, there's not much noteworthy that thrives here.

The Brassica (mustard) grew taller and bushier these past few weeks, its bright yellow petals giving way to the emergent seed pods characteristic of the genus. The leaves looked a little unusual, greatly lobed and deep green, different I thought than the usual jagged true leaves of the Brassica. But, I thought there are many species of them, and this one simply had the look of most.

I passed by the barn today, checking on the peppers which have barely taken hold in the cool weather of the prior week. The Brassica was still thriving, yellow flowers in bloom at the same time seed pods poked upright like small fingers pushing upward. Curiosity drove me to take another look, and I reached down to pluck a small cluster of leaves with their flower stalk to take indoors for identification.

Where the plant split easily at the branching stem, what's this? Yellow liquid oozed out onto my fingers, turning slightly orange upon contact with the air. Strange, for Brassica has mostly clear fluids within.

I brought it in, took out the wildflower book, and found its match . . . Greater Celandine. The yellow juice was the give away, evidently popular at one time to treat warts, according to the text. The text also indicated that Celandine is fairly common in New England, particularly in moist areas like my barn side. All this time I had mistaken it for mustard. Now I know not to confuse common this with common that.

June 18

The birdsong has quieted somewhat in the morning pre-dawn now that so many have gone to nest. Our little wrens must be getting close to hatching, and then the racket will start anew all day long. Wren chicks are particularly insistent, calling stridently from within the box, while mother and father busy themselves endlessly going out to forage and back again.

The robin chicks fledged two days ago. In the morning, I peeked within the burning bush when mother was away, and two babies sat quietly looking at me. The two barely fit in the nest, and it's a wonder that they could get any rest inside. By the afternoon, I looked in again, and they were gone. I wonder if one of these two fledglings will return next year.

Finches, catbird, oriole and grosbeaks have become less frequent; the latter two may be leaving soon for the higher elevations of the mountains to spend the summer.

It isn't all quiet in the morning, as the cardinals, doves and woodpeckers are fine with announcing themselves. Even the blue jays seem to be returning more frequently now.

It is the night which is becoming more active, with the sound of crickets and grasshoppers calling, and the occasional dove or owl thrown in the mix.

June 19

Bindweed is growing quickly now and is particularly noticeable in the yard periphery, snaking its way outward toward the light from within any bush or tree that gives it purchase. It seems to grow inches per day reaching and twisting itself vine-like taking over in its zeal to expand.

More interesting is to watch its progress where it grows in the ditches or roadsides, away from any would-be supports. Here, the plant will grow upright, rising several feet in the air on its sinewy vine, all the while searching for the chance encounter with an innocent branch or fence so that it can begin its climb in earnest. Look carefully here to spot a grouping of isolated bindweeds, where several have clung to one another braid like to make a stalk that reaches ever higher. It is ingenious.

Virginia Creeper, which is a bindweed, is close to flowering now. Cousin to the Morning Glory, its buds are fat near the old stack of logs in the side yard, where it has steadfastly climbed a young cherry tree nearby and now rests its bulbs on the top of the pile. Tomorrow perhaps they will open to display the deeply fluted white flowers, and I will be hesitant to keep up my vigorous battle to cut and pull this invader from our yard.

Pulling is rather temporary, of course. The orange colored roots are long and hardy, and inevitably two things will occur. One, you will break a root at some point underground as you lift and pull. Two, you will certainly fall on your backside, landing hard and covered with loose soil you've dislodged. The first results in new growth soon thereafter. The second results in wounded pride.

Summer

Maturity

June 20

We had a beautiful sunrise this morning marking the longest day of the year, our summer solstice. Seen from the top of the small hill that fronts Anna Maria College, the sun crested the eastern trees at roughly 5:20 am and at 78 degrees or 12 degrees north of east, according to my compass. From here onward until December, the sun will slowly begin its southward march, rising a fraction of a degree closer to south each day. Its best not to contemplate December just now, when the daylight is long and warm and life giving. It is a time to celebrate, as has been done for generations, that growing is upon us, the harvest is around the corner, and the darkness and cold are fully at bay.

We are not really "closer to the sun," as is so often misconceived, though logic could lead to this false conclusion. It is true that technically our present inclination puts the northern hemisphere several hundred miles closer to the sun, but this is inconsequential compared to 93 million miles that separate us from each other. It is the directness of the incoming rays that determine our seasonal warmth, indirectly speaking!

Ironically, the Earth's orbit is elliptical, albeit slightly, with the sun at one foci and the Earth in orbit around it. Presently the Earth is at the farthest point, or apogee in the orbit, making our North American summer coincide when we are most distant from the sun.

Regardless, we march along adding one day after another, shifting on the axis that balances our daily whirl, moving round and round in orbits and in circles of life and death, season into season.

Celebrate this.

The sun set today at 314 degrees just at 8:20 pm, a beautiful orange yellow glow that settled below the field to the west between the spruce line across the road.

June 21

Just after sunset, in the periphery of the yard, where the woods begin, the fireflies are beginning to flash. It is tentative now, with only a few early callers, though it will progress each night for a couple of weeks as more join in signaling to one another.

In the waning light, it is enjoyable to chase them, with jar in hand at the ready to hold them. They are tricky to capture, a flash there . . . run over to where it occurred . . . nothing, but a little further on . . . another flash. It is a game of chase we play, regardless of one's age.

We are fortunate to have these yearly harbingers of July, for I understand that the firefly populations are diminishing in places of the country where they've been established for generations. No one is certain, but hypotheses center on global warming shifts, urbanization, and over use of herbicides. These are the usual reasons trotted out to account for the notable loss of biodiversity within the past twenty years.

Bioluminescence is the term for the creation of light by an organism. Fireflies and glow worms are the most commonly known terrestrial examples, and there are numerous aquatic organisms that engage in it. It is a cool light, meaning that no heat is produced to speak of, unlike combustion with which we are most familiar.

Like most bioluminescent organisms, fireflies use it for signaling a mate, where the female "calls" in a particular pattern, recognized by an attendant male who signals in a different, yet familiar return. In the enveloping darkness, I imagine males and females signaling and searching, each playing their own version of firefly tag.

On a given night, there may be more than one species, and this is where things get interesting, as the signal calls are species unique. Photuris species signal in a given pattern, and Photinus species have their own. Imagine this as you observe the back yard, when dozens of fireflies are signaling. It is difficult enough to search for a single firefly, let alone discriminate between competing patterns.

It is here that mimicry also takes place in a fascinating way. The female of one species mimics the mating pattern of the female of the other species, for the purpose of luring the opposing male. Upon being duped, the male finds himself attacked and killed by the assassin female in her way of furthering her own species. Amazing really.

The light is created by a protein contained in the abdomen of the beetle, called luciferin. When luciferin is combined with another protein, the enzyme luciferase – which cuts luciferin, a chemical reaction takes place that releases photon energy (light).

All of this is happening in the backyard just now, and we will enjoy the show for the next few weeks.

Notes:
Bird's foot trefoil going to seed
King Devil and Orange Hawkweed going to seed.

June 22

Opening day.

There is more green now in the rows of the farm, as lettuce is ready to be picked, the tomatoes are mid-calf high and barely flowering, the peppers and eggplant are filling in nicely, and the leeks have finally seemed to come into their own.

I walked down to the lower portion of the front field, past the small stand of birch that guards the unused cultivator which has been fallow for several years.

Here the rows descend slightly toward the north wall, where Scott's bees reside, busy now with frequent comings and goings of workers bringing pollen to the hives from all corners of the field. These rows contain peas this year, greens and sugar snaps mostly, and they also are assuredly ready for picking, even though the white blossoms predominate within.

I bent down to the first two sugar snap plants and picked five pods, placed them in my pocket, and proceeded up the diagonal two track that bisects the upper and lower fields, making my way back toward the store. Midway up the tractor sounds became noticeable from across the divide to the west and south in the field planted with corn this year. Someone, either Fred or Larry, was out cultivating between the rows.

I stopped at the garage (which also serves as the store), though no one was about at this hour of the morning, and I stayed just long enough to write a note and leave two quarters. The note read,

"Sold on this opening day, five sugar snaps to Eric Howe for the sum of fifty cents."

June 23

At Martha's Vineyard

A southerly breeze came from across the ocean blowing directly up the slope of the beach off Katama Bay. The wind is building now, making cross lines on the swells that themselves will gain in size as the day passes, rolls that will turn to breakers in the surf pushing the sand up and back with wave upon wave.

In this morning light, the ocean is still a blue grey color but will change to deeper hues of navy and aquamarine as the sun climbs. Waves beyond the break line a mile or so off the shore catch the sun, and from our vantage they sparkle, mirage like as if heat were rising from some asphalt road several miles out.

Though low in the sky, the sun provides warmth enough, helped by the southerly wind. It is peaceful here just now, before the crowds arrive to spend the day.

June 24

At Martha's Vineyard

Island crows congregate in the morning within the black oaks that border the yard next to the house. Just like our summer residents in Paxton, the birds here now seem more idle and given to mischief, squawking to one another teasingly in the predawn and setting the otherwise calm atmosphere on edge.

The first miscreant arrived at 5:00 am, landing near the top of a particularly tall oak, in a branch that suspiciously arched its way back toward the bedroom window. "Caw caw caw" came the noise, rapidly and in staccato. Then again, and again. This was followed by several arrivals, sparking a series of guttural exchanges and gossip so as to wake the neighborhood.

June 25

The roadsides are being mowed today in our area. We heard the cutter moving slowly down the road up from Sunset Lane, the yellow tractor with its outrigger arm reaching over the top of the tall grasses, weeds, and wildflowers that have filled in the shoulders and ditches of the road. It is a primitive looking machine, with rotating chains affixed within a bulbous housing on the end of the arm, lowered so that the movement mashes and threshes plant and shrub alike.

We could smell its coming soon after we heard it, for the slight southern breeze carried all the scents of crushed foliage and stems, volatiles that spoke of shredded greenery – a decidedly Earthy yet acrid smell.

It is a necessary thing to mow the roadsides, lest brush and vine creep ever further toward the road, but I miss the tall grasses gone to head, hawkweed and vetch tucked within, and campion just now, let alone the creeping vines and poison ivy.

The noise is a nuisance as is the shredded devastation the roadside will bear for a few weeks until new growth takes hold. It will assuredly be green again in no time.

Mr. Cournoyer remembers when the roadsides were cut by hand, done by the Urbanovitch brothers years ago, with scythes in hand they'd spend days moving up one side of the roads then down the other, sweeping back and forth.

I imagine the cut look, where weed and grass lay flat, newly shorn and more tidy than the threshing they receive now by machine.

June 26

Chicoree is just going to flower in the ditches along the roadsides that have yet escaped the town's cutting. There are only a few blossoms here and there, but this mini heat wave we've experienced will hasten their development. Soon there will be a dozen or so on the each plant, opening in the morning light to reveal their beautiful blue purple coloring and aster pattern, set within the corded array of its green stalks and leaves.

The chicoree is a true summer flower, whose color is nearly unmatched in its clean resemblance of a summer sky.

The root is evidently edible, at least dried and ground, it makes a coffee substitute. I've not tried it directly, but I have sampled the New Orleans version, which is derived in part from chicoree root. It is a unique and somewhat acidic substitute.

June 27

These past few weeks, young skunks have been testing their newfound potency, usually at some point during the hours before dawn and often somewhere next to the house. I'm told that such skunks have yet to develop the muscular control to use their weapon appropriately; rather they experience a measure of incontinence, so to speak, at the slightest provocation, be it real or imagined.

Now that the nights are warm, we prefer to sleep with the windows open and fans circulating to deliver relief from the contained heat of the day. There's the dilemma; imagine sleeping blissfully, only to be awakened by the incoming smell of the potent spray from somewhere outside. Sometimes, it is possible to taste it, much in the manner of a passerby who wears far too much perfume or cologne.

Compounding matters is that skunks are largely corpunctular (a word I learned from a skunk enthusiast), which means they forage mostly at dawn and dusk – just at the time our dogs need to heed their own nature's call.

June 28

Many summer wildflowers have appeared within the past week in the successional transition from the cooler days of early June to the sultry beginnings of summer. Here is a brief report of what to see:

Travel down Route 56 toward Leicester along the reservoir, and look for the white blossoms of the Tall Meadow Rue, which seen initially may look like clusters of Yarrow to the passing eye. The Rue is decidedly taller, and the flower heads are feathery white poms, and the leaves are small trefoils.

Where 56 turns to Marshall Street, look to the north side of the steep incline, a favorite spot of mine for early spring wildflowers like Trillium and Adder's Tongue. Now, the roadsides contain both Smartweed and Swamp Candles. The former is also called Lady's Thumb, and the latter as Yellow Loosestrife. All along Marshall, in the sandy soil that borders the road, look for the purple heads of the Wild (or Blue) Toadflax, smallish stalks of 8-10" high with a few snapdragon-shaped tiny blue flowers at the tip.

Look to the borders of any yard or barn to see the tall heads of the Common Mullein now in bloom, with small yellow flowers that appear daily. These giants are often cut down in the leaf stage, mistaken as weeds like plantain when they are still quite young. The adult leaves are similar to Lamb's Ears, soft and greenish gray, with fuzzy hairs that cover.

Fallow fields may contain Black-eyed Susans now. There is a nice grouping by the old farm house on South Road out of Holden. This stretch has always been a favorite for nature preservation. From the point where South intersects Route 31, the road travels initially through a tunnel of the trees, with roadsides left undisturbed. Roses still flourish there in late June.

The road descends slightly and into open field land, before turning to the east and dropping sharply toward the reservoir below. Look to the "s" bend as the road winds downward, and see the gate that fronts the access road to the wetland. It is covered now with sweet peas, hundreds of pink and white hoods amid a mass of deep green foliage.

Sweet peas remind me of the dusty gravel roads of my Michigan summers, when the heat would dry the roadbed so, that passing cars would trail clouds of dust which would settle on the weeds and flowers by the side. We'd walk the road as children, bound for the general store with dimes or quarters in our pockets to buy penny candy, then back again through the pea-lined two tracks, all mixture of sandy road and green plants with pinks and whites throughout.

Notes:
Day Lilly in full bloom.
Coreopsis in full bloom.

June 29

For the past week, the wren parents have been frenetic during the day, both making unceasing trips to the woods and back to find food for the chicks inside the box. It is an interesting thing to watch; both leave, and the box becomes instantly quiet. A few minutes pass, and one or both parents return, either alighting on the box roof or the small branch just overhead. Regardless, no sooner do they arrive then a small cacophony of chirping begins, insistent and shrill. Mom or dad enters, and the sounds quiet to small peeps. Then the parent emerges, and the whole thing begins anew.

On a whim, I waited until both parents had departed, then I moved silently over to the noiseless box. I reached up gently and tapped my finger on the roof, and the chicks within started their calling.

Today however, the box has been quiet all day. At some point yesterday or the day before, the chicks must have fledged.

Notes:
Sundrops and Evening Primrose in bloom

June 30

June is at an end. It has been a month of green growth and vibrant song, of field flowers on display amid the grass grown tall in the full day sun. It's seen new birds taken to wing from nests built in trees and shrubs we've come to expect. It has perfumed us with the fecundity of pollen in the air, of still nights where the scents of honeysuckle waft slowly by. It has seen our longest day come to pass, and June knows that we will pay for this leisure in six months hence.

It ends with the first hints of change. Look closely now. The oaks and maples have leaves that show blight, curled and yellowed. The vegetables are growing yet, to be sure, but there is also fruit on the vine, expanding each day as maturity nears. Crab grass is taking hold in the yard, thriving in the hotter days and warm nights that will mark July.

The rush of May and June is over, and things seem to be waiting for July to arrive. The pace will continue to slow, as the heat builds all the while the days slowly begin to soften.

July

July 1

Pre dawn was notably sultry, and in the gray haze of the morning a cricket was chirping incessantly outside the bathroom window from somewhere within the rock wall that fronts the porch walkway.

I counted 178 chirps in one minute, then went to consult an old folklore almanac which lists how to tell the temperature from cricket chirps. Take the number of chirps per minute (178), divide by 60 (2.9), then multiply by 14 to get the number of chirps in 14 seconds (2.9 x 14 = 40.6). Finally, add thirty to this number to derive the outside temperature (= 70.6).

According to our arthropodial forecaster, the July morning was starting off warm and steamy. Sure enough, the outside thermometer on the kitchen window read 70 degrees. If July begins this way, it may be very hot and humid by the end.

July 2

Rabbit's Foot Clover is growing in the roadside ditch of Route 56 at the crest point where the airport runway is visible off to the east.

I also spotted at this same location the first Monarch Butterfly of the season, with wings spread wide in the morning sunshine, seated atop a tall grass head. The timing seems about right, as the milkweed has matured to flower and is now perfuming the air with its sweet scent.

Look for signs of the Jewel Weed in the shady hollows. There is an emergent grouping on Nanigian Road, midway up on the east side, just past the stream that runs through the culvert underneath the road. It is cool and moist here, conditions ideal for the orange blossoms of the jewel weed, with its succulent stems and delicate leaves.

Jewel weed is also called touch-me-not, which is an apt name once the flowers go to ripened seed pods in the fall. At the slightest touch, they really do spring open, throwing seeds in all directions.

It is a bit early yet for jewel weed, though we'll see more throughout the shady parts of town as the next months unfold toward autumn.

July 3

Queen Anne's Lace is starting to go to flower, with its broad nest-like cluster of miniature white atop a singular stalk. Seeing this invariably reminds me of my mother describing to me its namesake. As a child, I believe Queen Anne's Lace was the first wildflower to which I became familiar, no doubt on account of the story.

The common version is that the queen was embroidering lace when she accidentally pricked herself, drawing a single drop of blood. This is represented as the small cluster of deep red petals in the center of the field of white. Look closely over the next month, for the red develops as the white unfolds.

St. John's Wort is also proliferating now. There's a nice grouping in the undeveloped fields at the top of Highland Street, and I've also seen it growing along the roadside at the lower end of Grove, just before it meets Pond Street.

St. John's has tight clusters of yellow flowers, sitting on stalks that have small leaflets coming out from each axial node, giving the green an almost feathery look. The petals are a brilliant yellow, nearly an inch across, with dozens of stamens protruding from the center point.

Its distinguishing feature almost requires a strong lens or loupe. I use a 30x loupe, which is easy to carry and hold just above the petals. On the outer petal edge is a remarkable line of small black dots, nearly invisible to the naked eye (and surely indistinguishable to the middle-aged eye), and they remind me of the small blue eyes of the scallop, which are visible in the margins between its shell halves.

July 4

In Michigan

At noon we gathered at the Mercke House that sits high on the bluff, where the open front porch and yard overlook the expanse of the lake. Generations of families assembled loosely outside, young and old reacquainting with friends and reminiscing of days and years past.

The sunshine glistened on the lake, and from this height it was easy to spot the shifting winds, patterns of darkened water which moved across the surface along with shaded areas of cloud cover that made a patchwork of light and dark.

We are celebrating here, as we have done for over forty years; family and friends present and many only in memory, sharing our lives and our commitment to this place and this time, yet paying our deepest respect to the liberties that we enjoy.

Shortly, Nat reads a portion of the Declaration, and the faces of the crowd register a mixture; the adults are somewhat reverent, while the children fidget and giggle at the reading, some resorting to playing tag or spying upon one another.

I have witnessed this same scene for over forty years, and my own giggles of long ago have been replaced with a profound sense of appreciation. As Nat reads, it is easy to become distracted from the words, and I scan the faces of people I have known my entire life – friends who have grown older with the years, and children who are yet the next generation. The reverence I feel at this moment is enhanced by an overwhelming sense of belonging, to these people, to this place, and to these rituals.

July 5

In Michigan

In the stillness of the oncoming dark, after the wind
has calmed, and we sat enjoying a few quiet moments
before turning in, two loons began calling to one
another in their mournful way. They must have been
fairly far apart on the lake, for the first call came from
off near the eastern shore, closer to where we sat than
did the answering cry, which came a half a minute or
so from the opposite direction and more distant.

Their daylight call is the trilling familiar laughter, and
we see them occasionally out on the lake, usually
alone and away from shore. They will dive and swim
if encroached upon, and it is remarkable the distance
they can travel underwater, head reemerging on the
surface hundreds of feet away.

July 6

In Michigan

Today was the perfect summer sky, from sunrise to
sunset, the color and clarity of which we only imagine
when the steel gray winter skies take hold.

The sun rose at 6:20 am, which is notably later than
our Paxton time. It is diorienting to be in the western
edge of this eastern time zone, and particularly so far
north in latitude (Michigan is roughly 46 degrees

north at our cottage, while Paxton is 42.5 degrees). The net effect is a later rising of the sun but a notably later setting.

The sun crested just above the sweet grass field that predominates the old MacArthur farm here, a slightly hazy red glow, made so by the humidity of the dew emanating from the fields. We stood to watch its rise and caught a glimpse of two sandhill cranes silently making passage within the grass, stopping only once to squawk a warning cry at our presence.

Throughout the day, as the sun arched across, the sky became a deeper blue and uniformly so, with no clouds at all to mar the range from horizon to horizon. As I write this, the sun is closing within a few degrees of setting, and the sky has taken on a yellow and orange halo near its point of exit. It is nearly 9:00 pm, and the twilight will linger for almost an hour past, gently fading and giving way to the summer stars – Arcturus first over head and then Venus above the western horizon, still rising to its apex hence.

It will be crystal clear this evening, and the stargazing should be sublime.

July 7

In Michigan

Midsummer is well underway, yet there are signs that this season has begun to wane.

The roadsides here are fairly uniform with a mixture of native grasses, now gone to seed head and occasionally releasing clouds of pollen when disturbed. Dotting the roads and fields are the Ox-eye Daisies, and small Campions, Wild Carrot, Yarrow and Milkweed now in full bloom. Some portions smell summer fragrant, with the mixture of milkweed and sweet grass hay.

Growing quickly within, however, and nearly knee high are the Golden Rods. They are fairly nondescript at this point, with no evidence of the yellow plumes that mark late summer and early fall, but nonetheless they slowly progress toward maturity. Their coming is a signal of summer's own twilight.

Notes:
Creeping Dogbane in Bloom

July 8

 In Michigan

Another harbinger of things to come, a singular cicada called tentatively this afternoon from somewhere high up in the tall white pines that border the lake.

Earlier, I waded out into the water to cool off from the summer heat, and while walking out through the sandy bottom, waves gently lapping at my waist, I happened upon a young cicada which was struggling upside down on the surface. It was trying desperately to right its wings in order to dry them and escape.

I reached down and cupped both hands underneath, gently lifting upward so that the insect rested gently in my palm, allowing itself to go upright and crawl slowly onto my pinky finger with its wings properly folded backward on its body.

As I walked slowly back to the dock, the cicada rapidly beat its wings, not to fly or call out, but I suspected only to hasten their drying. It was only when I tried to coax it off my finger onto the dock post that it began to protest, making the distinctive rasping noise somewhere within its diminutive body. It was like having the clarion call of late summer in the palm of my hand.

Notes:
Yellow Goat's Beard in seed
Swamp Milkweed in Bloom
Cattail in Bloom

July 9

In Michigan

A warm and gentle rain fell today, a truly summer rain without the windborne front or violent storm. With a slicker and mud boots, it was perfectly pleasant to walk the two-track road and admire the effects of water everywhere.

The rain must have begun overnight, for the puddles in the low spots of gravel in the road were already full this morning, making the depressions look like miniature brown colored kettle ponds seen from high overhead; the sparse grassy ridge of the two track was the imaginary forest that divides them.

The surrounding trees were bent lower to the road, burdened by the moisture, and in several places the effect was a canopy where the boughs of one tree on one side met those from the other. Every leaf and needle had miniature droplets, and when any breeze stirred they collected and fell through the boughs making a sound like a rain chime.

Where the road departs from the cottage fronts, it makes a bend upon itself in a place where the canopy opens, permitting more sunlight. Here, just at the ditch edge where the gravel meets the mixture of wild grasses, heal all, Queen Anne's Lace, and creeping dogsbane, I noticed plump red raspberries within. They are full this year on account of all the moisture, and I stopped to sample several, picking them off the rain-soaked bushes and putting them in my mouth one-by-one. This very spot I've known and enjoyed berries for over forty years, and I recall walking to this bend as a child in summer with pale white bucket in hand to pull berries and place within for eating.

Notes:
Purple Coneflower in Bloom.

July 10

In Michigan

White clover is blooming in the roadsides, as are thistles. The white clover resembles tiny loosestrife, and the leaves smell vaguely like vanilla when crushed.

The second cut of hay was made yesterday at the farm and now sits in rows in the field drying in the summer sunshine until the baler can be put to service. Midsummer sees round bales nearly everywhere these days, but we worked the fields thirty years ago with square bales (which were rectangular really). In the sunshine we'd ride on the unsteady flatbed, pulled behind the Oliver tractor, two of us with hay picks in hand to catch and position the bales thrown up to us from below. When the tiers became too high, an elevator was hitched to the flatbed, lifting the bales up six to seven tiers and dropping them over for placement.

This second cut seems early, but perhaps the rainy June has hastened its growth. There is clover and vetch cut within, and the cows enjoy the additive all the more.

Notes:
Wild Bergamot and Bee balm in bloom

July 11

In Michigan

Perhaps there is Karma.

It must be a mast year for cicadas (I think the 17 year
emergent is indeed this year, though the apocryphal
predictions of cicadas blanketing everywhere simply
hasn't happened). Still, there do seem to be more
adults just now, and the trees have what appear to be
greater numbers of molt casings upon them. We have
yet to have the chorus calls that hallmark their full
maturity, and I am thankful at this point; cicada calls
mean the ending of summer and the coming of the
fall. As it is, this season has gone too quickly, and
there is still much to savor. We do hear sparse calls in
the afternoons now, furtive still as if testing their
ability.

I went out on the lake in a kayak this evening, making
my way slowly to the middle a mile or so out then
back, simply to enjoy the calm of the water and to
watch the water striders dance on the surface.

I was distracted more by the cicadas that were
floating upside down on their wings, still alive
through given to exhaustion. There were two dozen
or so on my paddle out and back, and I felt compelled
to stop, lower the paddle underneath the insect at
each instance, so that it could right itself, and lift it to
the rear of the boat. There it would shake its wings

vigorously for a moment before sitting still in a perch on the side.

By the time I returned to shore, I had over a dozen still sitting on the back. Some had taken flight during the return trip, making a buzzing sound while lifting off and heading out overhead toward the shore.

July 12

In Michigan

There are trails here that wind from one cottage to the next, sometimes down to the shore. The woodland paths have been trod for generations, traversing small brooks that outlet from the lake and navigating over tree roots and mossy stretches, where the coolness of the canopy affords a pleasant walk when the summer warmth has set in.

These are the trails of my childhood, where freedom and exploration began out the doorstep, as I sought out my friends down the shore to share in my summer adventures.

There were secret paths that we created, made by forays into some hidden fort within the trees or to access the beach, shell strewn and in the company of emergent frogs.

Many of these paths have vanished with the years, and even some of the main trails have gone fallow with the passing of generations. It seems that children explore less outdoors, and the highways of my own use are returning to the wild slowly, most only a memory now.

July 13

Midsummer perfumes are almost overwhelming just now. In winter, the senses long for some semblance of life and renewal, when the forceful wind carries virtually no scents. Spring's awakening spoke of Earthly promise, of moist humus and rain-covered roads, turned fields that would one day deliver provender enough.

Now we are awash in the scents of maturity, content that the promise of spring has been fulfilled, delivering us from the isolations of our winter hibernation. Here is a sample:

Milkweed continues in full bloom, and when combined with the clover and hay grass creates a unique sweetness.

The dark forests wasp balsam and fir, which mix with the cover greens of ferns that thrive in the shady coolness.

The farmer's market displays blueberries, raspberries, and peaches, each worth their appearance in taste and smell.

The warm water wind picks up the scent of rush grass and cattail, shoreline beach where small periwinkle shells create a thick line just a few feet on shore as the waves break.

Somewhere distant a cookout is happening; the smell of something on the grill floats by, and our mouths water thinking of a summer barbeque, complete with watermelon and lemonade.

July 14

In the wet areas, whether along the roadside or near a pond, look now for teasel heads. They are a finicky thing and prefer fairly wet and yet sunny locations, which is why they frequent the in-between ditch of some divided highways in the state or the accompaniment of cattail and reed grass at shore's edge of the lesser ponds.

Teasels must be close cousin to the thistles, for they too are beginning to bloom in the fields and waste lots.

Often, the easiest method of locating teasels is to simply seek out the sere heads from last year, dark brown with the distinct teasel leaves and prickly comb. When driving on potential roadways for teasels and thistles, it is the sere cluster from last year that advertises the spot. This year's growth is light green, with small purple flowers that grow in a curious ring in the teasel head, lifting ever upward toward the tip with each passing day.

I'm told the sere heads were used as wool combs long ago, and I believe it. They are prickly things.

July 15

A July heat wave began today, with temperatures in the low 90s and the humidity on the rise. The tractor was out early, well before dawn, and it's a wonder how they survive the long day in the fields, where the demands of cultivating and harvest are now in full measure. We'll see Fred still out working well after sundown, where after I imagine he simply collapses into bed. These days are the demanding stretch, which will intensify when the corn is ready for picking. This should be any day now.

We have a large patch of Coreopsis in the knot garden, in full bloom and exposed nearly all day to the sun's intensity. It seems to thrive in this heat, and there is something about it which reminds me of a folklore remedy the southerners used years ago to counter the summer swelter.

Old homes in the deep south had shallow niches just outside (and often around) the window sills, where the residents would take Spanish Moss from the trees and line the niches. The moss would absorb humidity from the passing air, providing a measure of relief, in the days well before air conditioning was invented.

Our coreopsis reminds me of this; its interior is akin to a dark forest, and the temperature within is some ten to fifteen degrees cooler and less humid on even the most blistering of days.

We don't line the windows with coreopsis, nor do we have a natural (or electronic) means of air conditioning. It's hot now, and we make due with fans at night, resigned to lying atop our sheets, thinking about the coolness that autumn will bring.

Notes:
Joe-pye weed in bloom along bend toward Hill Road from Whittenmore Street)

July 16

Warm evenings have intensified the mosquito hatch, brought from rains of a couple of weeks ago which filled the low areas enough to favor the larvae. The ecologist will argue the importance of this insect in the scheme of the food web, perhaps going so far as to postulate a possible keystone role; I am of two minds on this. The naturalist in me retreats in this discussion, and the selfish resident takes over. In short, I would eradicate mosquitoes for a week, were it in my power.

Fortunately, our evening denizens are at work. Just after supper, the dragon flies take to the yard by the dozens, flying in curious "Z" like patterns with repeats, at a height of ten feet or so. They remain for an hour or two, till the twilight descends, giving way to our more secretive crew.

We have several bats that live in the attic vents, easily visible in the daylight as brown balls of fur wedged tightly within. On the whole, they are quiet during the day, apart from a chittering sound when disturbed. At dusk, they emerge to hunt, and we enjoy watching them flap about, locating insects with sound and performing their acrobatic maneuvers to adjust their flight.

Just now the oaks are dropping leaves, sparsely so, to accommodate the loss of water transpired by the high heat. We find some on the ground with small, unfulfilled acorns, and this is particularly so if a wind storm has brought down any small branches with leaves. These acorns are our natural projectiles for playing with the bats.

We collect the acorns and wait until the bats fly overhead, then toss up a single nut high into the air. It is truly amazing to watch the passing bat abruptly change course, dive toward the falling acorn, perceiving it to be an insect. All this occurs in the stillness of the twilight, apart from the gentle flapping of its wings and the nearly silent clicks and squeaks of its radar.

Notes:
White meadowsweet in full bloom

July 17

The garden has been pathetic this year, and I fear the heat and drought have taken its toll. July can be cruel this way, particularly since we vacationed away at the cottage earlier, when the July heat beat down on the garden, left to fend for itself.

May saw enthusiasm with transplanting of seedlings, the promise of maturity seemingly likely. June's rains tempered the growth, but it provided moisture enough to facilitate the warmth that we knew would come.

Come it did, and full force no less. The garden I left at the start of July has been replaced by wilting plants, with little to show, replete with the thriving purslane and chickweed among the stalks.

Now we cultivate and water, hopeful for progress. The tomatoes still have flowers; the cucumbers will recover, as with the squash. Only the peppers seem unperturbed, though well behind where they should be.

Notes:
First Goldenrod in Bloom at Highland Meadow

July 18

Late June's deep greens are slowly giving way to a maturity that brings fading to more yellow hues. There is still green enough, to be sure, but it is unmistakable that the pace of production can only be sustained so long.

With maturity comes the first hints at decline, and the leaves of oaks, maples, ash and willow all show signs of fading color. The vibrant green of June now shows patches of wilt or yellow.

Yellow and orange will explode of course, when autumnal change takes hold and the trigger moments of cooler temperatures and fading light arrive. Now, the yellows are a normal succession, and indication of fatigue where the frenzied pace of production must wane.

There are other yellows to be found, which will become more abundant these next few weeks and herald the ending of summer. The golden rods are beginning to bloom, only here and there just now, but surely more tomorrow.

These pennants of late summer fill the fields and roadsides well into autumn, and will juxtapose with the New England asters to display our fall yellow and purple.

There is a small clone blooming today in the meadow on the circle of Village Drive near Highland Street. I noticed it standing amid an array of Timothy Grass, wild carrot, waning red clover, and daisy fleabane. On the whole it had a decidedly summer look – a meadow untouched, save for the hopping crickets, buzzing dragonflies and my passage within.

Still, the presence of the Golden Rod bloom was a reminder, that one season is giving way, slowly to be eclipsed by another. We tend to characterize summer followed by autumn, as if discretely to occur. Look closely; the change is already taking place. With passing days, the autumn that will be is taking hold of the summer that was.

July 19

Ascend a few thousand feet, and the relative rarity of the atmosphere helps with relief from the summer swelter. From the farm parking lot, you can just see the top third of Wachusett Mountain rising above the tree horizon of the lower fields. It is tempting to escape to the mountains today, ten miles as the crow flies or twenty via route 31 as it snakes its way through Holden and Princeton.

The view from the top is worth the trip, as much as the respite provided from the heat. We've stood at the summit and looked back toward home, trying to locate the farm fields as a reckoning mark by which we might know where home and friends remain. We even once jokingly asked Fred to wave to the mountain, knowing that we were to stand on its summit and send our own lofty tidings his way.

Our winter tendency is to draw within, to stay close to hearth and heat, where comforts of family and friends are less bountiful though more focused. Summer motivates its own scales, where the sights and sounds and smells of maturity invite us to sample all that envelops us. There are wonders here, both small and large – wonders from the intricate pattern of a spider's web caught backlit in the morning dew, to those of a grander scale, of tall grass rippling in the midday breeze, with the mountain that rises overhead in the distance.

It is a comfort to know that as our scales broaden with our exploration of this maturing season, we still take stock in looking toward home, perhaps in measure to reassure ourselves of our familiar securities, but perhaps also to simply look for others whom we might encourage to celebrate in our experiences.

I am thinking particularly of these things today, for at 5:27 pm the Cassini Probe is scheduled to look back toward Earth from a point near Saturn's rings. It is to take a photo of Earth from so very far away, and I plan to celebrate both my being here and its being there. I may even wave hello.

Notes:
Sweet Corn is ready

July 20

The sumac candles have been flame red for several days, and they remind me of the holidays, where deep evergreen boughs are topped by ornamental balls of red or even the occasional cardinal perched up high and within.

There is a cluster by the barn that is now at full height, twelve feet or so, having several main branches that are remarkably straight with palmetto-shaped leaves that reside on top. A few years ago, I cut down a dozen of the stalks and stripped them to dry, using an old draw knife to remove the outer bark.

A month later, we used these stalks to make walking sticks for the scouts, covering the sanded surface with a coat of amber shellac. They were remarkably pretty.

Each year, new stalks grow, pliant through May and June, growing ever taller and hardening all the while.

July 21

We've had seven days of unrelenting heat and humidity to rival the record books, so it seems. Officially here, according to the meteorologists, a heat wave requires three consecutive 90 degree days, and our seven puts the emphasis to it.

It has taken its toll on the bluegrass and fescue, both looking burned and with the ground rock hard underneath. Only the witch and crab grasses seem happy, giving a mosaic appearance of light green patches amid the yellow lawn.

Overnight temperatures have remained in the 70s, and with the tropical air in place the yard dews with moisture early and remains through the night. Near the three oaks out front by the road, our yearly mushrooms have exploded in seeming delight at this weather, and there are caps of several colors and sizes dotting this area.

A front finally arrived late afternoon, bringing tropical downpours and violent discharges with gusty winds that hallmark the changing of air masses. Tomorrow is to be cooler and less humid, and we are thankful for a change; we New Englanders wilt easily in this southerly weather.

Notes:
Sunrise at 80 degrees (10 degrees N. of East)

July 22

In marshaling evidence in support of natural selection, Darwin writes of the prolific degree to which organisms of all kinds produce offspring. The argument claims that the world would soon be overrun should all the progeny and subsequent generations survive from a single parentage. Thus nature is daily scrutinizing and on balance selecting only those progeny, all things being equal, who have some advantage be it small or great.

Take the wild columbine as an example. The dried seed pods are brown now and pointed upright so that if you grasp the sere stalk and gently shake it, the sound of a rattle is made. I placed my hand underneath a single pod and bent it with the other so that the seeds fell into my palm in a neat pile. I counted nine coal-black seeds the size of small peppercorns. A little arithmetic assists the example. There were 18 total pods (in clusters of 3 or 4) from the entire plant. 18 times 9 equals 162 total seeds from this single columbine. If all the seeds were to successfully overwinter and germinate next spring, the knot garden would be overrun. Let's assume that last year's columbine also similarly produced 160 or so seeds. One evidently survived, making the likelihood of survival a meager 1 in 162.

Dandelions must assuredly be less, with their silken blowies everywhere in late May. I wonder about the maple keys or acorns, particularly in those mast years when production seems to be in the thousands.

It is a wonder we have columbines or dandelions or oaks at all.

Notes:
Bouncing Bet (Soapwort) on South Road in bloom.

July 23

Yesterday, I said to Sarah, "Have you seen any hummingbird moths yet?" for we normally have a few by now flittering above the knot garden. She hadn't, and I was beginning to think we'd miss a year.

Today, I caught the movement of one out of the corner of my eye, flying quickly among our many pink phlox blossoms. The other appeared, and they shared time sampling phlox and white loosestrife, seemingly unconcerned with each other.

Rarely do they land, and the time spent at any one flower is ephemeral – a quick placement of proboscis and removal, as if merely having a brief taste of what nectar dwells within. The calyx of the phlox is rather disproportionately long (approximately 1 to 1.5″), and the moth must have quite a lengthy tongue itself to compensate.

The real wonder is its wings, for in one species they are transparent across a large portion, and for what purpose I can only guess. I photographed one sampling the phlox, and the image captured its wing in still, revealing the beauty of its mosaic design.

Notes:
Yellow Tansy in Bloom

July 24

I opened the sunroom door this morning to discover that both bird feeder poles were bent straight over to the ground, and one feeder itself had gone missing entirely. The dogs padded out in my wake and immediately became curious of some foreign scent in the vicinity, both noses to the ground weaving about. Tag paused just once to look up with what appeared to be a quizzical expression, as if he were to exclaim "what in the world is that?"

I suspect there's been a black bear come up from the lower woods, intent on easy pickings from the black sunflower seed and suet cakes, which we keep well stocked. There have been several sightings of bear in Paxton over the past couple of years, which isn't too surprising given how the town sees fit to allow more woodland acreage to be cut over to development.

The same city folks who then move this way, desirous of life in the country, will undoubtedly complain about the intrusion of wildlife in their yards. Such is the hypocrisy of things.

We have town members who serve on committees charged with preserving the open space and agricultural heritage while at the same time they advocate for the destruction of such land to accommodate unnecessary senior housing complexes. Were it not so irreversible, it might be pathetically comical.

I put on tall muck boots and a mesh shirt designed to confuse the deer flies and headed down the access road toward the lower woods, intent on finding the feeder. No such luck, though the suet holder did turn up a hundred yards from the house.

How the bear managed to ferry that feeder across the berm, through the tall brush, and to Lord knows where I will never know.

Notes:
Pokeweed in bloom

July 25

The produce across the road is a bounty for area deer, much to the Cournoyer's dismay, who are at wits end. Nothing seems to be immune, as peppers, peas, cucumbers, squash and beans have been notably affected.

Our access road is a natural corridor, as the deer come up from the lower woods to feed, usually around 10 or 11 pm and again in the early morning. I have rarely seen deer in my pre-dawn walks, so I suspect that they frequent the fields between 10 pm and 2 am.

Tonight may be such an evening, with the full Buck Moon rising late evening, and warm temperatures which will assuredly create a fog over the cooling fields.

We hear them occasionally, moving tentatively up the corridor through the grasses that have grown uncut in the two-track of the access road. On still nights, the rustle of their hooves and chittering calls of alarm signal their passage; we need only wait several minutes then look out the front window to see ghostly shapes making their way slowly up through the front yard, under the apple tree (a favorite respite in the autumn, when new apple falls occur), and across the road to the spruce line.

If the fog is just right, their evanescent shapes lose substance as they enter the fields, making their way to the lower rows beyond, melding into the mist.

Notes:
Rose of Sharon blooming
Sun Drops and Evening Primrose blooming

July 26

Early corn has been ready for a little over a week, thought we've waited until now to enjoy the harvest. There has been a sign up in the store, just above the cash registers, that alerts customers to the fact that the "early ears are small," something to which we've become accustomed through the years. Best to wait until the maturity of a week or so shows through.

Today we purchased our first ears, butter and sugar variety that is unshucked and freshly picked, with ears that are modest, though not of the size we will find in a month. It is a hallmark of our late July, to walk home in the summer sun down the farm driveway and left onto Grove, all the while slowly pulling away the husk and throwing the sepal coverings into the tall grass.

By the time we reach our driveway, the silks have been removed and the stalk stubble has been cut, broken clean by grabbing and yanking downward with a force.

Seven minutes in the pot and a few to cool. No butter or salt, thank you. This corn stands on its own, and we dream about it when the winter months set in.

July 27

Sarah purchased a new tube feeder, to replace the old one stolen by the bear last week. I've made several trips down the access road and around the berm, and have simply given up looking for the old one. The feeder was dark green, which matches perfectly to the low brush foliage, so for all my search it may be sitting camouflaged close by. Finding it can wait until autumn, when the living green has faded, as have the mosquitoes and deer flies.

The new feeder is evidently well received. As I write, there are six birds feeding (4 female finches and 2 male yellow finches), 2 birds in wait at the top of the shepherd's crook, and a cardinal and male grosbeak on the ground below.

The grosbeak looks young, perhaps a fledgling that is beginning to molt. His black back and emergent red chest are pocked with tufts of grayish white fluff, and the color is faded. The cardinal is striking as ever.

July 28

The breeze is gentle today, just enough that it is noticeable in the delicate birch leaves, which move in independence from one another so that the effect creates an almost shimmering look to the tree. These leaves are like tiny hands, waving about in the most subtle of winds.

The birch leaves will show the autumnal change before the others, though less dramatically so. When it is time, these leaves will slowly turn a yellow shade, all the while continuing their playful motion. And then, almost as one they will descend, as if exhaustion from months of summer dance has taken its toll.

July 29

It is virtually impossible to walk down to Asnebumskit Pond to inspect the wildlife without looking like a man possessed with fits. I can only imagine my appearance, seen from a distance, as I flail my arms about, occasionally cursing obscenities and smacking my head.

I mentioned deer flies several days ago, and they have been particularly bad this year. The wet June is now showing its harvest in full, including a mosquito boom for good measure.

Deer flies are notably insidious, and we seem to be suffering far longer this summer than normal. There is a growing part of me that wishes for a hard frost to take care of this problem, though I imagine the farm might object to this solution.

Our desperation foments all kinds of creative solutions, and here is a sampling of what I've seen around town:

An easy deterrent is to hold a fern branch in one or both hands, waving them about the head. Alternatively, I've come across hikers who resort to sticking a branch or fern in the back of their cap, with foliage pointed upward; the deer flies are prone to be attracted to the highest point of the moving object.

Once I saw a jogger with a blue plastic cup sitting inverted on top of his head, several flies affixed to the cup and several others flying nearby. (I later learned that Florida researchers have evidence that deer flies are partial to blue, and that a quirky home remedy is to coat a blue object with sticky substances).

More common is to dangle a bandana behind the hat, covering the neck which is so very subject to attack.

These are all indications of our New England desire to shoulder onward and enjoy what little summer Mother Nature affords us, even if we look ridiculous and unstable in the doing.

July 30

Thinking more on nature's evolution and the maturity of the season. It is a wondrous thing really, all that is contrived to achieve the possibility of reproduction. All the energy and intricacies in every living thing, and there are abundant examples now, in the backyard or garden or fence row.

We have a single golden rod clone which has been an interloper to the front knot garden. It poked its way up through the coreopsis within the past month, survived being pulled by the gardener's hand, and now is displaying its plumes of newly emergent flowers. They are tiny yellow things, though under a 30x lens they appear as detailed and large as a mustard flower.

The wonder is to consider that this single clone had 9 sub stalks, and each of these had approximately 9 stems where the flowers reside. I counted 56 yellow flowers on one of these stems. Conservatively, an estimate is 9 x 9 x 56 = 4536 flowers in this rather diminutive clone, each bearing the possibility of reproduction, if conditions favor.

July 31

July has come to an end, and the waning of summer will commence these next few weeks. The real work is beginning at the farm now, and it is impossible for them to keep up. Apart from the tomatoes, potatoes and leeks, which should be within the next few weeks, nearly all the crops have ripened, and there is a seeming endless series of trips to and from the fields in the truck.

As I write this, there is the truck now visible through the gaps in the spruce line, making its way toward the store from the lower field, backlit from the descending sun, and set in a fuzzy halo from the dust that is stirred up along the two-track as it moves along.

The lower field has corn, and the store will be needing fresh bushels, staying long enough in the back room to be graded before making their way to the shelf, where waiting patrons anticipate the arrival.

July has been this way, all hurry up toward maturity and wait with anticipation and with satisfaction.

Notes:
110 cricket chirps this evening with a thermometer reading of 59 degrees.

August

August 1

The ponds and lakes have changed notably these past few weeks since I last visited. Even the two-track access road is showing late summer's untidiness, with tall grass everywhere in seed and dead falls here and there which have been left uncut. Most of the wildflowers that line the sides have gone, save for the wild carrot that thrives in the few sunny spots where the canopy thins. The fall asters are bidding their time.

Just before the road ends at Asnebumskit Pond, tucked to the side and slightly within the low area of woods is one of Paxton's few certified vernal pools. Last time I was here, the water was seeping from the pool across the road via a small ditch that had been created by erosion. (The dogs are used to this obstacle when we walk in the spring, and I smile at their steeplechase leap across to avoid getting wet.) Now the pool itself is nearly dry, which is the norm for August. The teeming sounds of spring peepers and wood frogs we enjoy so in early spring have receded, yet there are crickets in full.

There is still an abundance of life to be explored, and on occasion I'll take a small vial full of the remaining pool water home to put a drop on a slide. A microscope reveals a complexity of plant and microorganism life that is simply wondrous. There are creatures here that have intricate adaptations for survival.

Asnebumskit is showing its late fall appearance. The reed grass and rush sedges are tall, as are the cattails and golden rods that line the northern shore. Though it is called a pond, it must be deep enough; plant growth goes out only so far, and the deep water areas are free of both plant and algae. Shallow ponds, like that of Thompson Pond or Streeter, are filled now with a mixture of water lily cover and duck mill, and algae bloom. The latter seems thicker in Thompson, I suppose on account of the fertilizer run off from the houses that border its edge.

August 2

The farm has learned from its sources that western Massachusetts is showing signs of blight in both tomatoes and potatoes, and of course the fear becomes that it will find its way here.

It is an irony of late summer that we desperately crave frontal changes to bring much needed moisture for the maturing fruit, yet more often such storms can also deliver unwanted pests and plagues. An early hurricane in the south will push all sorts of insects ahead of it. Easier yet are windborne spores of fungus that can settle here on the fields.

There's no report from the forecasters about coming storms in the next few days, though that doesn't slow the preventative work here. The tractor was out early as usual, but the normal diesel was masked by the fans of the sprayer, working the tomato rows with fungicide.

Notes:
Cardinal flower and Pickerel Weed – in bloom in the wetland bogs of Rutland rail trail.

August 3

One mile south of town on Route 31, just after Keep Avenue where the road gently curves to the right on its way toward Moore State Park, there is an open field which is beautiful just now in the August sunshine.

It is sun dappled at 9:00 in the morning. Yellow greens of the uncut tall grass are dotted with thousands of Queen Anne's Lace. With no distracting homes or structures in the midst or background, this field is simply idyllic, almost a romanticized version of a summer pasture in full maturity.

In passing by I stopped to estimate the flower count, for the shear number of the spreading stalks is incredible. In one square meter quadrat, I estimate 6 individual lace plants. The field must be nearly a ¼ acre, and there are 4840 square meters to the acre. 4840 times ¼ times 6 = 7260 plants in this relatively small plot.

Each composite flower is a world unto itself, and seen in isolation resembles an enlarged snowflake with the florets as patches of crystals in arranged patterns. A sample flower contained 38 small clusters, each lifting upward and supporting a platform of florets of roughly 36 tiny white flowers. 38 x 36 makes 1368 florets on the singular Queen Anne's Lace.

This ¼ acre has thus by estimation 1368 x 7260 = 9,931,680 tiny white flowers spread about, each a potential awaiting chance and circumstance to be pollinated.

The number is overwhelming to me, a reminder of my own relative insignificance in the spatial sense at least. There are dozens of fields like this in Paxton and dozens of small towns in New England so alike.

These flowers live and reproduce and die, in so many fields; their ubiquity is the norm at this place and in this season, and we who tend to believe in an exaggerated sense of ourselves in this land should pay greater attention.

August 4

A couple of weeks ago, I took a dawn reading, measuring the compass point of its rising in order to compare it to the solstice figure. Part of the impetus for doing this is because it has noticeably become darker in the mornings when I've awakened, and the sun seems to be setting much earlier. Of course, this is to be expected, as we are shifting ever onward toward the equinox some six weeks hence, yet the new darkness still catches us off guard.

The sun rose at 80 degrees on the compass, or 10 degrees north of due east. We've lost 2 degrees since the solstice, and this had made the difference. From this point, we will accelerate our daily loss of light until the equinox, when, though we will continue to lose light until late December, it will at least lessen its pace.

August 5

Look to the wetland bogs or slow-moving forest streams, where the canopy is thin so that the sunlight comes easily to the ground. It is here that favors the striking red cardinal flower, which is in bloom this first week of August in this region.

Its color is truly like no other, and cast against the background of greens of other foliage or varied blue of the waters around which is thrives, the red petals appear blazing and out of place.

The first time I saw one was years ago in northern Michigan on the Ingleside Road out of Douglas Lake, at a point where the dirt road crosses a broad meadow stream. The water was shallow, tannin-colored and slowly moving with a sandy bottom and small grassy island of sweet grass and Timothy. It was at the edge of one such island, that a tuft of cardinal flower was on display, and from the passing road with the sun striking on full, it gave the impression of small fire bursts in the background.

That was years ago, and I've looked to find the cardinal flower here in Paxton to see its brilliant colors again.

Today, while riding on the Rutland rail trail, just past the deep ravine cut where the bedrock is exposed from the blasting done years ago to create the passage, a ¼ mile further going downhill is a bog section, open to the August sun. As we rode past I caught a glimpse of fiery red sitting just at water's edge near the trailside. Cardinal flower flourishes here amid pickerel weed and water lily. It is worth the trip to see it.

August 6

In the building light of the moments before the sunrise, on the eastern horizon the star Sirius now makes its appearance. It is just visible for a few minutes and then fades as the dawn's approaching light becomes too strong. As the weeks progress, this star will precede the sunrise ever earlier, and we will look to its brilliant blue sparkle in the dark skies before dawn.

The ancient Egyptians looked to its summer rising as a harbinger of the annual Nile inundations, and they celebrated its coming. They also associated its arrival with the sultry heat of late summer, a time when lethargy took hold in the midst of the day.

Sirius was known as Caniculus, which the Latin associative is Canus, or dog. It resides in the constellation Canus Major, or big dog, and its summer arrival we associate with our "dog days" of August.

Indeed, our own two Westies seem to know that the dog days have arrived. In the middle of the day they have only the energy to trot to the middle of the yard and lie down on their sides, tongues rolling out loosely and bellies moving quickly up and down.

August 7

No sooner do the dog days arrive then does an unusual clipper front follow, bringing a taste of autumnal crispness. Temperature this morning was 49 degrees, and there was almost no humidity throughout the day. Add to this a constant wind from the northwest, and it simply felt as though we'd made an overnight transition to fall.

In truth, this change was refreshing and even welcome, particularly since we know that the heat of August will return in full measure. Soon enough, we will accept these days of coolness, letting go of the summer that was and preparing both mentally and physically for the winter that will be, several months hence thankfully.

Today's respite is simply that glimpse, and we prefer to look at it as the benefit of autumn's promise. The air is invigorating and fresh, with clouds taking on well-defined shapes off the horizon. The haze of summer with its lethargic quality has retreated, if only for a day or two, and we can glimpse the coming of fall around the corner now.

August 8

Gold finches are mating this month, which is atypical of our dooryard birds. We're accustomed to the flurry of birdsong in the early mornings of April and May, and it is odd to see such activity in August. Our tube feeders remind me of busy airports, with constant occupation at all openings and a half dozen finches either perched on the shepherd's pole crook or flitting nearby a feed opening in hope of dislodging a companion.

The finches time their mating season with the coming of the thistle seed, and the correlation this year seems right; there are thistles and burdock in abundance in the undisturbed fields that border the college and the farm.

We have none here at the house yard, so our finches resort to the purple cone flower and echinops, both which have seeds that in some respects resemble thistle, though without the downy tufts.

Our front knot garden has dozens of plants for them, and a small depression nearby in the driveway asphalt holds left over rainwater enough that the birds can whet their thirst after eating. They are pretty little things, the gold finches, perched at the edge of the small puddle, brilliant yellow cast in sharp relief against the dark of the asphalt, bending down tentatively to drink.

As I write this, sitting in the afternoon sun on the back porch, I count 18 finches around the two feeders – 12 female and 6 male.

August 9

The sun crested the lower trees at 6:45 this morning, high enough to bathe a good portion of the back porch in golden light. It was fairly warm out and with no breeze, making the old Adirondack chair we keep a perfect spot to simply sit and awaken.

I dream about these mornings, when winter sets in full, and this very spot is covered twelve inches deep with crusted snow pack. The enjoyment then is of a different sort, where such austerity and elemental harshness is indeed invigorating. It is only a detached appreciation at best, seen and felt beneath a layer of insulation we've steadily accumulated since last autumn, both of the physical and mental kind.

To sit here in this summer morning is an exposed investment, where the warming sun and verdant scents are nurturing and inviting to be a part of the experience.

Tendrils of steam drift upward from my coffee cup, sitting now on the arm of the chair, and their shifting presence has attracted a curious hummingbird. She hovers frenetically near the cup, if only for a moment, so close to my still arm that I feel the small wind her wings create, before she quickly departs to sample the nasturtium blossoms nearby.

August 10

Fred was out in the field late afternoon walking
slowly up a singular turned row, pushing an old
hand planter. From my vantage point, it was a
timeless image, of farmer and antique implement
working to plant radish seeds in the soil in
preparation for a possible late fall harvest.

It is easy to imagine this same tool used in this same
way and in this very field by his father and his
father's father, the continuity of a commitment to this
life and this place, the cycle of the seasons played out
over years of plantings, growth, and harvest.

August 11

The swamp maples in the lower valley that forms the
basin of wetlands toward Moore State Park are
beginning to turn. We've had successive cooler
nights, and I suspect this has prompted their
changing color, as the low areas are cooler all the
more. The road that travels from Paxton toward Barre
(Route 122) crosses the wetland, and on the east side
the maples that border the small pond which feeds
the culvert are becoming gold and auburn, and when
seen against the background of the still green wild
grasses and low shrubs makes a nice transition
between summer and autumn.

It's a month yet before our sugar and silver maples
will make their change, but there is evidence now of

the progressing season. The sugars are starting to drop their keys, and we see them collecting in the shoulders of the road. A still wind yesterday brought down dozens, winged key seeds still connected at the fruit, the pair forming a little bow tie.

Over the next few weeks, those that remain high in the tree will drop further and separate, falling to the ground in spinning helicopter fashion.

August 12

Perceid Meteor Showers

I awakened this morning at 3:30 and saw through the bedroom window that the sky was crystal clear, perfect for viewing the Perceids.

Needing only a bathrobe, I tiptoed down to the sunroom, turned on the porch light to check for any bears, raccoons or skunks at the dooryard feeder, and looked once again to see that the sky overhead was clear.

Lights off, then to the porch to sit on the Adirondack chair, which was damp from a dew fall overnight.

Almost directly overhead, Cassiopeia sat in her throne, with the evanescence of the milky way barely visible against a sky slightly lit from the distant Holden lights. While I waited, small rustling sounds came from the direction of the lower woods, and the near constant white noise of cricket calls were in the background.

Then, a flash overhead, a small streak off to the east which started near the zenith and moved nearly 10 degrees across the sky. A minute later and another, followed quickly by two more.

August 13

There are showy goldenrod plumes everywhere now, and it can't be too long until the first hints of purple asters appear. In the unmowed periphery fields of Anna Maria, the goldenrod clones are particularly tall and healthy looking.

Now is the time to examine them closely for galls, visible as cancerous looking lumps in the midst of their slender stems. These were formed by the plant itself, in a bit of self trickery induced by a parasite that lives within, the gall fly larva.

When the plants were mere shoots in late spring, the gal fly female laid eggs on its exterior. The newly hatched larva secreted a chemical that caused the plant to develop the gall structure, in which the larva lives within in the soft plant tissue, while the exterior provides a tough protective layer.

In August, as the gall nears its full capacity, the larva too have grown within, spending a portion of the month chewing away a tunnel just to the surface (but not through) of the gall. Then, it settles down to ready for over-wintering, using the gall as a sheltered home.

In early spring, the larva transforms into the adult gall fly, piercing through the thin remaining layer of the gall shell and beginning the cycle anew when the first goldenrod shoots arrive.

Look closely at the galls now; many will have drill holes pierced into them, made by birds like the downy, who have learned to seek out the larva within.

August 14

Not since the wood frog and peeper calls of late April have our evenings experienced such background noise. The orthopteras dominate the chorus, and their mating calls are simply the epitome of the sounds of late summer nights.

Grasshoppers make up the constant sounds we hear, high-pitched trills that seem at once to be close to the house and far away in the woods. Of course, they aren't really constant, but it is difficult, if not impossible, to discern where one insect pauses. There must be dozens that overlap, and the white noise sounds like the gentle intake of air through the mouth which is just slightly open and relaxed. It is a pleasant hallmark of August evenings.

Crickets keep a steady rhythm, and their familiar strident chirp comes frequently. Temperatures are warm this evening, and these black insects do synchronize to the ambient condition.

Katydids too are calling, through less often and less rhythmically.

It is peaceful now, in the gloaming as we sit on the back porch watching our two bats hunting overhead. The sharpness of the trees of the lower woods is lessening in the fading light, and the stillness of the night apart from the chorus is wonderful.

August 15

Older maps show the connecting road between Pond Street down at the end of Grove and the causeway over in Holden, and through the years we've seen many cars go down our street only to return shortly, when they discover its closure long ago. It was called Kendall Road, and now it is a fallow two-track that climbs out from near Streeter Pond and over the ridge line toward the Kendall Reservoir basin. There is a gate to prevent vehicles from traveling, and the land has been turned over to the reservoir authority as a protected water source.

We walked the old road this afternoon, admittedly well aware of the questionable legality of our doing so, but our intentions were less intrusive; we meant only to observe the neglected way, to discover the sluice that feeds Kendall Reservoir from Pine Hill, and walk the abandoned access that leads from the ridge saddle to the big dam.

This way has been abandoned for years, and the old road is fairly eroded, particularly on the descending hill to the sluice where seasons of rain and snow melt have created water channels and washouts. There is a remnant open field on one side, filled with early successional shrubs and trees and bordered by a stone wall. The other side is forest, rather thick and overgrown, and the contrast of open field sunlight on one side and darkened woods on the other is slightly disorienting, made more so by the interruption of light here and there where the canopy reaches across the road.

August 16

Thinking more of yesterday's walk. The sluice was fashioned of cement, roughly 3 feet wide with walls 2 feet high. It meandered the 1 mile valley that began at the Pine Hill dam and made its way down to Kendall reservoir. There was perhaps a half foot of flowing water, and we reached in to feel its current, watching bits of detritus flow past, having found its way in from the woods upstream.

A neglected asphalt road followed beside the sluice, both winding lazily uphill, and we walked the pavement toward the dam. It occurred to us how remote our surroundings felt, here not two miles from lower Grove and only a mile or so to Holden, yet we remarked that the valley and flowing water could have easily been within some idyllic expanse in the mountain country up north. It was so strange not to hear any human-made noise, and the old limestone walls of the sluice, weathered and ancient looking, added to our feeling of stumbling upon a lost civilization.

August 17

Rain came hard last night, followed by clearing that made the sunrise reflect off the water that still glistened on every surface. The humidity of the ground steamed in the building daylight, making a strange fog-like layer that ended about 6 feet high.

The water over the spillway at Moore State Park was flowing quickly on account of the deluge, and there was a fair roar of it as the volume made its way down the cascades past the old mill site.

The mill pond is particularly pretty now, with lily pads thriving and Joe Pye Weed and goldenrod thrust up on the near shore line. I suspect the pool was more stagnant yesterday owing to the drought, but the overnight rain took care of that.

The sandy path from the mill into the woods was still damp, and a few low spots had small puddles waiting to soak into the ground. Where the trail descended into the pine woods, as it formed a single track, the fallen pine needles were arranged in horizontal bands roughly 3 feet apart, evidence of an effluvial flow down the path making eddies of floating debris.

August 18

In the sandy roadsides
along back roads that are
less traveled, the chicory
is thriving now. In the
early morning, the
purple-blue of its flowers
are deeply concentrated
as the petals are together
like a closed umbrella,
waiting for the warmth
of the sun to fully open.

The color is no less
diminished in midday,
when the half dollar
sized flower is in full display, in clusters set within
the corded stalks. Few blues match the richness of
chicory, and even the cerulean sky of those summer
days where the humidity is so low that the blue
overhead is deeply concentrated, is less striking.

Along Nanigian Road, the chicory combines with
spotted knapweed, and the effect is a mosaic of
purple and blue splashes of color set against the deep
greens of the tall grasses and ivy.

August 19

My friend Bill is preparing this week for his new
elementary class to arrive soon, and we anticipate

school buses will be part of the routine again. My own classes begin at the end of the month, and I am both looking ahead and looking back. It is inconceivable that this summer will end soon, and yet there are signs enough that this is the case.

People speak of summers going by more quickly than they used to, and while we know that this physically isn't true, perhaps there is some sense of pace that we impose upon ourselves. It is tempting to be constantly looking ahead, to the next vista or the next day, to the appointments of tomorrow or the hopes that we work to achieve.

We've complicated our lives in our forward-thinking orientation, and for so many the pace is made ever quicker by the technologies we seem addicted to employ. These may indeed liberate us in one sense, but surely they detract from us in another.

August 20

Yesterday's entry needs more context, or perhaps just more space here for me to complain. We are slowly reaching the end of the one season where people can comfortably be outside at leisure experiencing the wonder of all things in all sensations. June, July and August provide variety in excess to ourselves, and we can enact with the natural world in so many ways as our own investment.

Yet more often I witness people engaging not with the reality that these days afford but in every sense virtually or artificially. They move about with smartphones in hand, less a part of their surroundings and rather in some distraction, likely trivial, and certainly artificial.

Why bother going to see the cattails, when they can be instantly accessed via a device? Why learn the catbird's cry, or witness the metamorphosis of a hornbeam? The stars can be seen at any time and at a finger's touch, so what is the point of a nightly display?

I swear, in this age of wonder, when information can be accessed at a moment's notice, when we can have satellites pinpoint our every step, when we have increasing difficulty in simply being alone, we have become impoverished.

August 21

An adult cicada lay dead at the end of the driveway, having no evidence of injury. It is if it simply tired and lay down to die peacefully. I am surprised we don't see more of them as such, for their afternoon calls are strident, surely requiring exhaustion to produce. We hear them now in earnest, beginning loudly enough as a buzzing call, then rising in both volume and pitch, often being joined in concert by a neighboring cicada. This lasts as long as a minute, until abruptly the calls cease, leaving a stillness that gives the impression that the insects are recharging.

This adult was large, perhaps the size of my thumb, with a whitish underbelly and dorsal surface that was a mottled green and brown. This camouflage explains so well that we often hear them if ever see them perched on the trees.

Its wings were striking, simply beautiful, folded backward to rest against its body, with deep venous lines that divided the cellulose-looking material of the wing proper. It reminded me of a stained glass window, absent of color yet no less intricate, as if by some design.

Notes:
Indian Pipe in bloom.

August 22

White asters all around, mostly the thin, white-toothed asters

The knotweed (oriental) is going to flower now, and in places the odor strongly smells of honeysuckle. It is a strange feeling to be walking nearby and catch a whiff of its perfume, thinking for a moment that early June has returned.

Honeysuckle is tolerably sweet, much like jasmine, but the knotweed's version is too sickly, as if honeysuckle nectar had started to ferment.

The knotweed is everywhere in town these days, and as an invasive it seems to thrive in Paxton. It is particularly bad along Route 122, just south of the public safety complex, against the guard rail that divides the road from the lower wetlands that are filled with cattails and red-winged blackbirds. The knotweed press outward into the road, making a nuisance for drivers and walkers alike, despite that the town workers cut it back weeks ago. It returned in earnest, and now is in full display of white flowers that resemble the stalks of wild white clover, yet knotweed's are situated in groupings, upright and in series.

I've read that it is proliferate via runners, and so it requires successive pullings over several growing seasons to starve its roots sufficiently. Mere cutting the foliage won't suffice, though it does provide a respite for a month or so.

August 23

Sturgeon moon. Sunrise at 6:05 at 85 degrees

At 5:00 this morning, the full sturgeon moon of August hung 30 degrees up from the western horizon, casting everything in the twilight that only moon reflection can create.

I went down to the stretch of Route 56 that travels from Paxton toward Leicester, skirting along beside the Kettlebrook Reservoirs that are nestled within tall white pines. The road was perfectly illuminated by the moonlight for the first quarter mile, until entering the canopy of pine, where after the way was made of trunk shadows and light.

It was beautiful here, moving along close to the reservoir and seeing the moon interrupted by the passing trees, crickets calling in earnest in the background, made bolder by the warm August morning and sultry beginning. It is what we think of as a summer moon, with light that diffuses more gently through the humid air, making everything it reveals softer somehow, as if it is important that these August days begin more lazily, not cast in sharp relief.

Even the moon itself has a fuzzy halo, so distinct from what we'll expect in several months yet, when crystalline skies reveal everything in harsher detail.

August 24

The temperature this morning was a cool 47 degrees, well below where things should be and a taste of what is around the bend.

Below the eave of a window in the back of the house, a small yellow jacket nest sits tucked within, hanging upside down so that the cells face open to the ground. It looks like a medium garlic clove, though the paper is grayer and the cells are only the size of a pencil eraser.

We normally avoid these nests in August, on account of the activity. Yellow jackets aren't as aggressive as the paper wasps or ground wasps, which will seek out intruders with a vengeance. Still, there's no sense in poking the bear, as is the idiom, so we keep a respectful distance from the half dozen or so nests that get established each summer.

This morning however, it was possible to have a closer look. The cooler temperature had slowed the yellows to the point of lethargy, and it was safe to inspect the nest despite the eight little demons that perched in stupor on its surface.

Their antennae were moving slowly, and when I breathed softly on the nest, several beat their wings rapidly in response. Whether this was a warming mechanism or simply an attempt at flight, I can't say, but in the process two of them dropped from the nest to the ground below. There they lay buzzing slightly, though lacking energy enough to do much more.

The remaining moved about the nest slowly, obviously agitated by my breath, yet the only response they could mount was to walk about to one another, touching antennae.

An hour later, I returned to inspect the progress, as the nest had been exposed to direct sunlight. Despite still cool temperature, the radiant energy was enough to liven the wasps to the point that getting too close became risky.

Notes:
Ragweed in full bloom.

August 25

The pace has slackened just a little across the road, now that all the late planting and transplanting has ended. The focus these past few weeks has been on corn, and the pumpkin truck (as we call it) has been making frequent round trips each day to Echo Farm to fill the bushels.

JD went today to lend a hand in picking, and I watched him climb in back of the pickup, stand on the metal flooring and hold onto the rough-sawn siding of the bed, grinning as Fred and Dan were seated in the cab. The trio drove slowly away up Grove, leaving me standing in the intersection of the driveway and the roadway, watching them move along.

I am pleased at his going, for his exposure to such work, hard and honest, walking along the rows with basket in tow, pulling and twisting the ears to break the nub. It is important that he do such things away from us and under the eye of one whom he so admires.

The ears have lengthened since mid July, and this late summer variety has more sugars for the flavor. To say that such corn is mouth watering seems insufficient and trite, but nevertheless it is a wonder. Now is the season for sweet corn and bruschetta, made with our own sun-ripened tomatoes and basil which have survived the July heat, only to thrive in this cooler August.

Soon we will start hoarding the corn, in the manner of the chipmunks and squirrels which are in earnest now as the acorns have begun to mature and even fall from the oaks. We'll cut the kernels from the corn after cooking store them in freezer bags, two gallons worth, and save them till sometime in winter when we simply need a reminder of summers – those past and those that will be again.

August 26

Off to the eastern horizon, Orion is now visible in the hour before dawn. This morning was unusually cool again and clear, making all the stars contrast well against the sky that hinted at morning.

Orion hasn't been a familiar since last February, when we'd watch its departure against the evening sky.

Just above and to the left of the shoulder star Betelgeuse sits Jupiter, clearly the most prominent object in the heavens apart from the waning gibbous moon that is nearly overhead. I recall Jupiter sitting over the right shoulder Bellatrix last

February, and so its slow revolution around the sun continues. It takes 30 years for Jupiter to complete its orbit, and so in a single year it will travel roughly 12 degrees across the sky. It's been a little over half a year since February, and Jupiter has moved about the width of four fingers from one shoulder of Orion to the other, perhaps 7 degrees or so. This seems right.

The last time Jupiter visited Orion was 1983, after which it made its slow progression through the zodiac, year-by-year, until coming full circle, of sorts. I am enjoying this now, for I won't likely be alive when it crosses Orion again next.

Notes:
First wooly bear caterpillar.

August 27

Cool again this morning for August, and this early taste of chill is starting to accelerate the autumnal changes just a little here and there.

The birdsong of June ended weeks ago, though since there have been daily greetings by the normal summer residents of cardinals, finches, chick-a-dees and such. But these calls have been morning greetings and sounds of daily business typical of late summer, less musical and varied than the mating songs of late spring.

This morning in particular was quiet, apart from the half-hearted cricket calls, tempered by the chill that dampened the grasshoppers. In the pre-dawn, it was so still that it was easy to imagine a killing frost had occurred, silencing all but the most hardy or lucky of the insect residents. As the daylight came and the air warmed, the birds resumed their conversations, and the insects rejoined in background noise, but things felt different, as if they all are whispering about change and migration soon enough.

Look now to the older maples in town, those who reached maturity years ago and yet continue to hang on each year in producing leaves and life, even if more of their limbs remain lifeless than not. These maples show the change sooner than do others, with chlorophyll degrading now and oranges and yellows beginning to display. The stag horn sumacs and poison ivy are also starting to change throughout town, the former particularly pretty with individual leaves on the periphery turning yellow and others yet a vibrant green.

The ivy yellows up the vine, which climbs the trunks of all the trees it seems. Soon it will make it appear as if the trunks are on fire, with speckled patches of brilliant reds and yellows ascending.

Notes:
Fireweed in bloom all along Grove upper and lower

August 28

Two of the yearly prognosticators have appeared, and as usual only time will tell if they are accurate, or coincide.

The grocery store contains the latest copy of the Farmer's Almanac, and I admit to browsing one for the winter prediction. This becomes an important topic of conversation this time of year, as we put to rest our summer leisure (farmers excluded) and look to the inevitable that will arrive.

I am particularly keen on this forecast, for I have yet to order a wood delivery, and the severity of the winter certainly affects the stock. We are low on hardwood in the barn, and it's time to get a cord or two (or three) of seasoned sticks dumped in the side yard.

The almanac forecasts a colder and snowier winter, and while we've come to expect a 50% accuracy in their predicting skills, much in the manner of the groundhog, it's difficult to ignore this forecast. A typical New England winter coming, full of everything and then some.

The wooly bear caterpillars are also out more conspicuously now. We've seen juveniles crawling about on the roadways and driveways where they are easier to spot. Folklore has them as a predictor of the winter severity, depending on the relative thickness of the black bands to the browns, or is it the other way around? Take your pick, I suppose, for like most such things, the evidence of efficacy is at best 50/50. Thus far, I've seen woolies with more brown than black and woolies with more black than brown, and I suppose Mother Nature is ambivalent about the winter and about the Farmer's Almanac this year.

Notes:
Boneset in flower

August 29

The giant sunflowers are still thriving in this late August warmth, and now the seed heads will begin to enlarge and droop as their maturity continues.

Louise cuts a dozen or so heads each morning and places them loosely in pale, white plastic buckets in front of the store. It is a pleasant contrast of the red store front with the white and yellow splash of flowers on one side of the open garage, and collected zinnias of all colors set in another bucket on the other side.

The finches and chick-a-dees will start to investigate the drooping heads, now particularly that the coneflowers and daisies have run their course. The fare is beginning to diminish with the onset of September around the corner, and the birds have increased their activity at the dooryard feeders. Larger flocks are becoming active, and we had twenty or so red-winged blackbirds descend to the ground below the feeders, mill about in apparent Tom foolery, and then depart suddenly and as one. Soon, they will begin their southern migration.

August 30

The old crab apple tree in the front has had ripened fruit for a little over a week, and there are several beneath its boughs, having fallen when the wind blows.

There are relatively few good fruit trees in Paxton to speak of, apart from the occasional crab or quince that serve more decoratively than functionally. I suppose we are accustomed to the convenience of apples at any time of the year and of several varieties from the grocery store, but I wince when I see their specimens, particularly in January.

Insecticides, fungicides, preservatives and genetics have been employed prodigiously to allow this luxury, and the store apples uniformly approach some Platonic ideal, at least visually.

The heat of July must have impacted our crabs, and the cool, dry August concentrated the sugars. They are smallish this year, no bigger than a golf ball, but they are unusually sweet. Best to inspect them all around before biting; more than half have already been sampled by bird or insect, and several have worms within.

Those already fallen will slowly decompose, and in the heat of the day they give a cidery scent to the surrounding air that combines with the increasing smells of tannin and nuts, and drying grass – the beginnings of autumn perfume.

August 31

August has come to an end, and summer is slowly being eclipsed by the coming of autumn. This past month as been cooler than normal, almost June like as far as temperature, making us more wistful about summer's decline. We so often suffer through the heat and humidity this time of year that the oncoming coolness of September is a welcome change.

No summer lasts forever, though we are trying to enjoy as much of its lingering maturity as we are able.

In the late afternoon, the angle of the sun has shifted so that it comes through a gap in the spruce line across the road, hitting the front of the house directly. It is pleasant to simply sit on the large granite boulder that serves as a step onto the front door. The rock is heated well in the sun, and it is inviting to just sit and listen to the waning day.

Cars continue in and out of the farm driveway, as they have all August, and sometimes we hear the muffled sounds of laughter or greeting from neighbors who have arrived by chance at the same time. In the distance, the sounds of some sports practice can be heard from Anna Maria, a reminder that the end of this month also means the beginning of school. Birds call here and there, tempered from a month ago but still conversational – a catbird by the arbor vitae, a dove startled from the roof of the barn, finches at the sunflowers in the knot garden. The wind gusts briefly, first noticeable in the spruce, then coming across the lawn, picking up the few early – fallen oak leaves and setting them in a whirl. The chimes tinkle behind me, and I hear Sarah coming out the mudroom door, screen door spring stretching and relaxing making its distinctive noise.

It is easy to enjoy this in August – to sit and just listen to all that lives around us. It is warmth and pleasure and life in the simplest sense.

September

September 1

If April is the time we begin spring cleaning, in anticipation of the warmth and freshness that summer affords, September is sadly when we begin to button up.

It is still warm out, which makes this preparation all the more bittersweet, knowing that our days of comfortable weather are nearing their end.

September is usually the time when the wood that was felled, cut and seasoned in the spring and summer sun is split and stacked into the barn. This year, I neglected to drop a few trees in the lower woods and thus needed to order a cord of seasoned hardwood. In anticipation of stacking, I went to inspect and tidy the area of the barn used for wood storage, which is also where we keep the snow blower, spare gardening materials, and cast offs from spring and summer projects.

Red squirrels had established themselves as summer tenants, building a nest out of fiberglass insulation in the eaves, taking the material from the adjoining junk room. After an undisturbed season, they made a mess of things, and there were nuts, grass, corn cobs and other detritus strewn about.

It took me the better part of an hour to clean, and only once did the reds chitter at me for disturbing their area. I did refrain from bothering their main nest up high, though I removed the rest of their mess.

Fortunately, nothing had taken residency in the snowblower engine cowling, and I suspect the naphthalene pellets I placed there last spring repelled the deer mice.

On top of the remaining stack of wood unused from last winter, I placed a rolled up sisal rug (just to get it out of the way). When I grabbed it to take it over to the adjoining room, a mother deer mouse plopped out of the end, several babies clinging desperately to her. I saw all this in the fraction of a second that it took for her to fall onto my sandal shoe. I heard a squeak, felt them hit my foot, then watched them launch into the air as I screamed like a little girl, kicking upward.

September 2

We ad a cord of wood delivered yesterday, and it took the better part of an hour and a half to ferry it from the pile in the driveway down to the barn for storage. It's a shameful thing to pay to have seasoned wood delivered, when we are surrounded by forest of hard and softwood in plenty, but there's no escaping the fact that we didn't cut and section our own this past spring.

This cord is a good mixture of oak, maple and hickory, with sticks of ash thrown in the lot. The latter we'll use to kindle, for ash burns hot and more rapidly than the other. It is all buttoned up well in three rows, each chin high and against the inner barn wall, where I'm certain the mouse family I displaced yesterday is already seeking another nest site within its labyrinth.

How long they'll remain here is questionable, for there were no seed stores to be found when I dislodged the nest yesterday. I suspect the mother deer mouse used the old rug as a temporary nursery, planning to vacate the barn soon enough when the babies were just a little further along.

Likely, we'll see and hear these same mice again in the walls and attic of our old house, when the frosts arrive that drive the winter mice indoors for comfort, unwelcome by me but appreciated by our cat, who has had to content herself all summer with watching the chipmunks and birds from within the sunroom porch.

September 3

There are asters everywhere now, particularly in the roadside ditches and open forest floors, along old stone walls, and sitting beneath field fence rows where fox tail and Timothy grasses reach high.

The toothed, white-tipped asters have been out for nearly two weeks, but they seem to have exploded in numbers just this weekend. They are so numerous in spots that when seen from a distance it is easy to imagine that some unusual dusting of snow has settled on top of the deep greens in which they reside.

They are a decidedly more ragged looking blossom, having the appearance that every other white petal has been removed, as if each were just used in a first round of "loves me, loves me not," with petals picked out in alternate. What they lack in completeness is made up in abundance, and like most asters they seem hardy in heat, rain, cool and wind.

The signature New England Asters are just beginning to show, with purple petals pushing through their sepal covers. I saw one in full bloom today along the Grove roadside; this early arriver displaying its purple coloring and yellow center. We'll see more and more as the days progress, and the depth of purple and contrasting yellow will be incredible. These we will continue to enjoy well into fall, past the first frosts and often into the initial snows. New England asters are hardy harbingers of autumn's coming and going.

Notes:
New England Asters beginning to bloom

September 4

Sarah saw two towhees at the feeder base today, black and orange plumage with their characteristic back scratch way of searching through the cast off on the ground. We haven't had them around since late May, and I suppose this in an indication of their autumn migration southward.

This morning was notably dark at 5:00, and this thought of transitions is certainly evident in the heavenly progression. The gloaming of dawn didn't hint until a little before six, and all too soon we'll accelerate further toward more hours of darkness.

Walking back home at this hour, the sky took on the iridescent purple, where the canopy of white pines overhead lay in sharp black contrast against the lightening sky. Crickets and grasshoppers were the only sound. There were no birds calling whatsoever, and their absence is a conscious reminder of the transition that has really been slowly happing since March, I suppose.

September 5

The peppers have been ready at the farm for a little over a week, though the heat and humidity of the past several days has certainly hastened their maturity. It's all Fred can do to keep up with orders from customers, particularly the Europeans, who favor the farm's pepper crop.

Bushels of colors sit in the store, making a pleasing display of greens, oranges, reds, and yellow, and we enjoy picking certain ones from the basket that have peculiar features which give them resemblance to something or someone. It is a variation of searching for shapes in the clouds above, enjoyable and silly.

September 6

Canada geese are on the move now, tentatively still
and not yet in the regular formations and frequency
that we associate with their migration. But we are
hearing a call from time to time, and loose gatherings
fly overhead to inspect the fields across the road.
Only a few days ago, Fred turned under the corn in
the field next to Anna Maria's cross, leaving the
ground uniform in its mixture of dislodged soil,
mustard and corn stalk stubble. In the mornings we
see geese browsing in this field, searching for fare that
is more easily accessible now.

This must be an ideal stopping point for the early
migrants, for there is plenty of fresh water with
Asnebumskit nearby, and the farm provides enough
varied fodder to fatten up the birds sufficiently. On
occasion, when I'm walking the dogs in the morning,
I release them from the leash so that they can satisfy
some terrier impulse to chase the birds, and it is
amusing to watch their two little forms receding
across the field, following the small flock which is
struggling reluctantly to take flight.

Yesterday, we stumbled upon what had the
appearance of a secret goose meeting, in the small
pond adjacent to the administrative house in the back
of the college. I had hiked down to see if the Joe Pye
Weed that rimmed one edge of the pond had yet gone
to seed, and when we crested the small hill that forms
a berm to the pond, we saw within at least 50 Canada
Geese milling about in the water. Given that the pond

is only at most fifty feed in diameter, it was an impressive sight of goose density.

Our abrupt intrusion startled several to the point that a chain reaction happened. Within seconds, the geese began attempting to take flight, churning the water and creating an unbelievable cacophony. We watched them depart, flying toward the lower fields which lay to the north.

Notes:
Phlox seeds popping.

September 7

In the heat of the day, the wild concord grapes seem to release their distinctive smell, and in certain places of town, the air is infused with a delicate smell of grape. It always reminds me of Welch's Grape jelly, which isn't too surprising, of course, but yet an important personal link to my own childhood somehow.

Odors in general are powerful things, stimulating not just our olfactory senses but also our memories in which they were a part. Spring has its verdancy, of Earthiness and water and new growth. Summer's fragrances are more sultry, the stickiness of pollens, the smell of cut grass and of barbeques, honeysuckle and of thunderstorms. Autumn's smells are all their own, of ripeness and of decline, the grape vines, apple cider steaming in a mug, the tannins of fallen leaves after a shower, the first hints of wood fires as the nights grow chilly.

September 8

Early cider has arrived at the farm, placed in half and full gallon jugs on the shelf where the apples, peaches, blueberries and grapes are sold. This early batch will be tempered in sweetness and slightly acidic, compared to what will be stocked later in the month as the apples continue to ripen. I like it either way, and so I brought home a half gallon, poured a mug full and heated it in the microwave. It was a delicious taste of fall.

I remember making cider years ago in Michigan, when as a child we'd spend an occasional fall weekend up north. Activity at the MacArthur farm had slackened since the frenetic pace of getting hay mowed, baled and stacked in the mow, and we kids could enjoy other work like cider making.

We'd take the truck to the upper field that overlooks Lancaster Lake, where several apple trees sat in uncultivated surroundings, though separated from the wanting eyes of the cattle by fencing. The cows would surely enjoy rubbing up against the apple trees to dislodge the fruit to the ground so they could gorge away.

We'd fill bushel baskets with apples, handpicked by standing in the flatbed of the truck and reaching high. In my minds eye, I can still see the cows looking expectantly across the fence at us, hoping that we'd allow them access.

We'd ferry the apples back to the farm, where Bruce or James would have the press ready, a medieval-looking contraption of slated wood and large turning screw. The apples were placed in a cheese cloth, then situated within the press. The screw would mash the cheese bag, and the juice would flow out the wooden sluice at the bottom into waiting glass jars, each filled in turn by a funnel held between the sluice and its neck.

September 9

The phlox seeds are reaching maturity, clusters of brown spherical pods that sit on top of the plants as remnants of where not too long ago their blossoms of pinks and whites lay resplendent for the hummingbirds.

Now in the warmth of the September sun, on particularly still days we have begun to hear them popping open, one or two every few minutes. The seed is flung wide, leaving the sere brown husk to fall lightly down to the ground.

Notes:
Pumpkins on display at the farm.

September 10

Kipper sits on his side in the sun-warmed driveway, enjoying the midday heat that with each passing day seems to be waning. His tongue lolls out to one side, and his chest rises and falls rapidly, though he seems perfectly blissful even on the verge of overheating.

Though autumn is my favorite season, there is a part that is bitter sweet. Perhaps it is because this time is really a signal of the beginning of the ending of this yearly cycle of growth to decline. We tend to notice these progressions more readily now, in the yellowed leaves that start to fall from the trees, hastened by crisp wind, in the call of the Canada Geese that fly high overhead, and in the field of ready pumpkins to be harvested next to the picked rows of sweet corn whose leaves are starting to decay.

These things we experience are indeed simply a part of the cycle of the seasons that have been and will be, with or without us. I have seen 46 such autumns, each unique in its own way and upon my own spirit, all governed by the same successional forces that allow one season to be eclipsed by another.

I think of these things as I watch Kipper in sheer ecstasy on the sun-dappled pavement. I wonder if he is already longing in some way for the spring or summer that already has been, or if he thinks about the waning of this season. Chronologically, we are both in the autumn of our lives, and I wonder if he, like me, has any measure of deep value of these passing seasons which are filled with anticipation and contentment and longing in varied measure.

September 11

In the uncultivated areas between the planted rows, and along the two-track road that provides access to the fields, Virginia Pepperweed is showing its seed heads in readiness. They are really quite an attractive thing as weed species go, with tiny seed flags in radial arrangement that rise up several inches from the basal plant which may yet be green. Most have dozens of seeds in each raised head, and their brown display resembles the shepherd's purse of two months ago, though the spiral pattern is distinct.

The name is apt, for the seeds are edible and do have a tinge of pepper taste. It's easy enough to grasp the raised stalk in one hand lightly, pull upward with enough force to dislodge the seeds yet not so much that the stalk separates. I'll collect fifty or so small seeds easily this way in one motion.

I've read that these were used in olden times as a poor substitute for actual pepper and that the seeds are a good source of vitamins A and C.

Notes:
41 cricket calls per minute at 4:00 am.

198

September 12

Two days of sweltering heat, well above normal for
this time of year, and we are thankful that tomorrow's
cold front will return things to the expected autumnal
feel. No one likes to be reminded of the summer that
just was, when we have mentally closed the books, so
to speak. To return to the heat and humidity of late
July is simply improper. It feels out of place, these
conditions, when the angle of the noon-day sun is
notably lower in the sky, the leaves on most
deciduous trees look tired and increasingly yellow,
and the asters line all the roadsides and fence rows.

The only benefit is that the heat has hastened the
ripening of the tomatoes on the porch, which had
seemed destined to arrest at green with the autumnal
chill the past ten days. With luck, we'll enjoy a few
more slices of beefsteak reds on our bread and cheese,
the bruschetta of late summer that makes the heat
worth it, almost.

September 13

Our twin black oaks in the front are dropping acorns
more frequently, making little noises in the grass and
on the driveway when they hit. And by no
coincidence the gray squirrels are spending more time
in this vicinity, picking up the newly fallen manna
from heaven and taking it to the horde.

These two oaks are curious, for by all appearances they are of the same age and located only twenty yards apart. Both are rather majestic as oaks go, rising nearly 80 feet into the air, with large spreading crowns whose leaves provide welcome shade in the summer months when the midday sun strikes the house and yard. If I had to guess, I'd estimate their age at 60 or 70 years, planted at the same time back when this section of Grove was a two-track dirt road that connected the Van Wyck Farm at the intersection of Grove and Route 31. I'm told that our property was formerly a potato field earlier in the 1900s, so its possible these two oaks were planted as some sort of road front.

They are curious, because their behaviors differ so with respect to acorn production. The southernmost tree is presently in a mast year, dropping far in 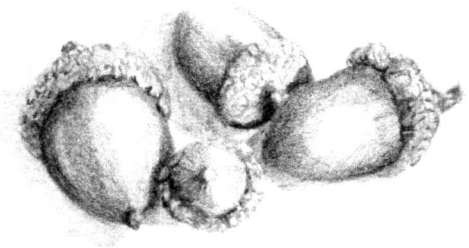 excess of its sibling and much more than I recall seeing last year. The northern twin is more frugal this year having been in mast the autumn last. The northern's acorns, regardless of year, are consistently larger, with fuller caps and slightly greener casings.

September 14

The town neglected to mow the roadsides a second time this late summer, and we have been treated to a display of wildflowers and weeds in more abundance along Grove.

Noteworthy have been the pileworts or fireweeds, which have risen high above the ground foliage and have for the past two weeks been displaying white seed heads. They resemble the dandelion heads in the manner in which they seem to "poof" upright, but they are decidedly more cotton looking, thicker and strikingly white.

Smartweed and jewelweed have also thrived, particularly in the roadside areas that are more shaded by the abutting forest. Jewelweed was so numerous only a week ago that it was almost disorienting in places to see such splashes of orange amid the delicate green.

Now, the asters are dominant, though their whites and purples are set within the varied tall grasses which have slowly been changing colors, giving any particular stretch a patchwork appearance of shades of green, yellows and even slight purple leaf blades, where seed-laden heads of all configurations rise upward.

The roadsides are simply beautiful now.

September 15

With the onset of cooler weather, I suspect there is some ethos that forgives or even excuses a separation from the natural world. It is too easy to claim the convenience of indoor pursuits, and the ever-present intrusions of technology in favor of the empiricism afforded by the outside.

Observe the masses in town, coming out of the bank, or standing at the soccer field, walking along the sidewalk, or waiting for a child to arrive on the bus. Electronic device in hand they detach to a virtual place, seemingly oblivious to the physical world of which they are a passive part.

It is too easy to lament the poor state of humankind's ambivalence to their natural surroundings. Put simply it is so very disheartening to witness such disconnect.

Paxton is no different than the next New England town in this way, or likely the majority of towns in these states. There is beauty so profound here and now, in the cycle of the seasons, and yet people have distanced themselves from being a part of it.

Notes:
Buckeye trees dropping nuts.

September 16

It's one thing to get caught underneath the black oaks unaware as the acorns drop, though they do sting a little. It's quite another to be near a hickory tree when they let go.

There are a couple of shagbarks in the lower woods near the vernal pool beside Asnebumskit Pond. They are fairly majestic looking, with steel-gray bark on big trunks that rise 70 or so feet into the air; the bark has the characteristic look of peeling, much in the same manner that shake roofs tend to gray and curl as they age.

Around the base of each are strewn the open husks of the hickory nuts, evidently having either been opened from above by the squirrels (who then cast the outer casings aside) or been dropped to the ground and managed from below. It's a dangerous business standing beneath these trees just now. The squirrels are up high foraging, and sure enough nuts of both types, opened and whole, come crashing down.

Whole hickory nuts are golf ball sized if not larger, and they would give a memorable knock on the noggin if the unfortunate were to occur. Their odor is pleasing, though decidedly piney and acidic, much in the way that black walnuts have a distinctive smell.

Our Michigan farm was called Hickory Ridge, for it was situated on the top of a plateau, the edge of which had nearly a half dozen old and large shagbark hickory trees, likely planted intentionally as a ridge line in the early 1930s.

These hickories were only a dozen yards from the house, and we enjoyed all manner of forest birds and beasts who made use of them. Particularly wonderful were the families of flying squirrels who made their nests in the boughs; we'd see them at nighttime, scurrying among the branches and occasionally taking flight from one tree to another.

September 17

It was cold this morning at 36 degrees an hour before dawn, with no humidity or wind to speak of. It looked and felt and even smelled like autumn approaching.

There was a slight wood smoke fragrance in the air, and I suspected the Cheney farm had started an early fire in the stove to take the edge off the chill in the house. Out in the street, where the vapor lamp shines down an amber-colored light, the smoke had collected in the low spot, settling in like fog seen sometimes in cooler valleys.

Approaching from up Grove, where the road rises slightly at the junction of Sunset Lane, Glen's twin headlights were visible just above the layer of ground smoke, and as his car reached the descent past the town fields toward the low spot, the sharp beams vanished and became a brilliant diffusion of light, each particle of smoke laden air reflecting in all directions, until his car glided beyond.

September 18

The cool nights these past few days have hastened the change of the crab and witch grasses in the yard, giving our front a more motley appearance. Soon enough, the summer weed grasses will die off, leaving patches of golden sere among the still green bluegrass and fescue that predominates.

I am admittedly hypocritical about this. I am pleased when the warm nights of July arrive, and the crab seed explodes toward new seedling growth. The crab is thick and limey green all July and August, giving our mostly unkempt yard a more respectable density. But it is a case of temporary embroidery, and like our summer songbirds which add color and beauty, the fall onset prompts their departure. Such is the lawn, where soon it will be thin again.

Compounding matters this year are the Japanese Beetle larvae, which have evidently taken residence and are doing their best to consume the tender roots of fescue and Kentucky. They've been slowly growing since mid summer, of course, but the damage is only visible now. It must have been the hot July, for I see such damage in several lawns around town.

September 19

We dodged a frost, but it was close. When I checked
the thermometer at 4 this morning it registered 37,
and by first light in certain places in town, roof tops
had patches of hoar frost, and a few of the lower
areas, like the large field midway down Grove (the
field that abuts the Leicester water stream) had bits of
frosty haze back lit in the tall grass and nested cups of
Queen Anne's Lace.

I'm certain the farm has been monitoring the temps.
One precarious dip too low would damage much of
the provender, especially the peppers, eggplant and
tomatoes. This is always the risky dance they play
each fall, wondering if the late transplants of May will
dodge the frosts of September.

Today is after all the Harvest Moon, and now that the
frost is more than just a "someday," the farm can hear
the ticking of the clock more earnestly. What began in
what seems so long ago as promise, and saw itself as
growth and then patience, is now resplendent as
bounty, but only if time allows. Spring was much of
hurry toward maturity, and it seems that now it has
become hurry to gather.

September 20

The just waning full moon hung brilliantly 30 degrees
up from the western horizon at 5:00 this morning. In
the absolute stillness of the predawn, two Great

Horned owls were having some conversation, perhaps about the beauty of the moon, which looked as if it were cut out of paper and placed on the purple iridescent sky.

At 53 degrees, it was perfectly comfortable to walk up the road, using the moonlight to see clearly, where the familiar trees, light poles and mailboxes cast moon shadows. The light was easily strong enough to read by, and in the quiet of the morning (apart from the garrulous owls) I was tempted to sit on the ground at the end of the farm driveway and read the paper that Glen had deposited sometime earlier.

Moon shadow is a pleasing way to experience the sun's light, but I'm told it is possible to witness Venus' shadowing. I suspect that it must be closer to the new moon when the skies are especially dark, the humidity must be low, and Venus must be relatively close (and high in the sky). Even then, it must take sharp eyes to discern the shadow of objects from the light reflected off Venus, but how wonderful.

September 21

We let the lawn grow long these past several weeks to strengthen the root stock (and because the dryness of late has made the growth sporadic).

Today was likely the last mow of the year, and the newly shorn lawn became instantly more yellow, as the lengthy green grasses have been duly clipped and mulched within.

The mowing was noisier out by the oaks, which have seen fit to drop copious acorns, particularly the southern of the twins as it is evidently in mast. Acorns would get caught in the mower frame and bang within while the blade spun mulching away.

Afterward, we were treated to a spectacle in the front; the lawn, now closely cropped, revealed two distinct quarter-sized holes roughly fifty feet apart from each other. Chipmunk den holes, and we had suspected the location of one, as the chipmunk would scurry to that general location only to disappear magically within the taller grass. Now, the hole is plainly visible, and as if on queue the chipmunk made an appearance from the garden, darting in a direct line toward the hole. Our dog Tag gave chase but was seconds too late as the chipmunk dove into the ground. Tag was resolute and stuck his white snout down into the hole, smelling so forcefully that we heard the puffs of breath and saw small clouds of dust billow around his face.

I kept expecting to see the chipmunk blow forcefully out of the neighboring hole each time Tag exhaled.

Autumn

Harvest

September 22

Autumn officially begins at 4:44 pm this afternoon, according to the astronomical figures in the Farmer's Almanac. Whether we like it or not, it is time to bid farewell to the summer, at least formally. The change from one season to another is a slow successional process, after all, and the evidence of summer's waning has been distinct enough the past few weeks.

The trees around town are showing signs of fatigue, with limbs that seem to bend lower, laden with nut or fruit past ripeness, or burdened with leaves that are given more to yellow and blight. There is still plenty of green yet, but it is far different from the vibrant hues of lime and Kelly which signaled the youth of months ago.

Tomorrow there will be less daylight than darkness, a celestial turning point in equinox that forgives the natural world to accept the fatigue and ultimate dormancy that comes on the heels of late fall. Tomorrow there will be more leaves in the road, newly fallen with resplendent colors and whirling about in wind carried dust devils. There will be gourds of all shapes and jack-o-lanterns, and bittersweet berries that ripen in beautiful reds against their orange husks. The purple asters remain, defiantly showy against the sere tall grass, made so by the frosts that have come early.

Notes:

Sunrise at 6:50 and at 106 degrees.

September 23

Down Grove, past Robinson's Greenhouse, as the road descends and the woods thicken on the western side, the forest becomes boggy, and there is a small vernal pool set back from the road on the eastern side, partially hidden by the brush and grasses that encircle it.

In the spring, this pool is a cacophony of peepers and wood frogs, and in the summer the red-winged blackbirds often congregate among the cattails on the far side.

Now, the pond is nearly dry as is normal for such pools, particularly following the prolonged arid stretch the town's experienced. There is just enough mucky leaf fall in the basin to characterize it properly as wetland, and I imagine that a little investigation would turn up several types of amphibians.

One such, a juvenile red-spotted salamander, was making its way across the road, heading from the area of the pool to some urgent spot in the lowland woods. What inner drive compelled it to venture forth I can only guess.

It was roughly two inches long from head to tail, a muted orange color, with slightly darker spots covering itself. Some time go, I suspect this creature was one of the many iridescent day-glow ents that we see in this area, no bigger than an inch.

I used a flat stick to lift it gingerly and moved it to the western side of the road, where it resumed its trek toward the woods.

September 24

The fallow hill between the farm and the college is at its most beautiful now. It is a small knoll really, unused in years past for cultivated growth, because it is likely a mass of bedrock just underneath the topsoil, and it best serves as a break between what used to be the flats below and the home above.

Seen from an easterly approach, the hill displays its fall colors in full measure now, Earthy tones that are warm and simply autumn like. The top is largely quake grass and crab, both showing purple hues hastened by the cool nights that quickly rob the summer grasses of their chlorophyll. Midway down is Timothy and Fox grass, which are yellowing and tall, swaying in the breeze in uniform waves that resemble puffs of wind that move across open water. Below them, where the neglected two-track cuts across where there is moister ground, green grasses of some sort still thrive.

From only a short distance away, it's easy to imagine this small hill as some far off majestic peak, where the distant bands of color represent changes in the alpine zones. Up close, the grasses each have their own character, and it is pleasant to traverse the hill, seeing the color and hearing the sound of the wind rustling in the sere blades.

September 25

There was a mild frost this morning, visible only on the tops of the cars that had been left out overnight in the common area beside the church. The lawns and rooftops seemed unaffected, so the temperature must have been somewhere between 33 and 35 degrees.

This early frost ebbs and flows like a slow moving tide, coming in stealthfully in the early morning, in the low lands initially before progressing further each day, until it takes hold fast, and we see autumn depart.

After the sunrise, this frost will retreat, leaving wet car tops and dew-soaked grass in its wake.
September 26

Some of the burning bushes are starting to show spectacular color, with small leaves that have gone to a deep crimson. In a breeze, these leaves flutter about, giving the bush an appearance of fire, when seen from a distance (and with a little imagination).

I would plant more of them, were my conscience not overruling, as burning bush is listed as invasive. This does seem to be the case, for there are more of them in town now than I recall from years ago. A proper census is difficult most times of the year, for apart from their bladed stems, the bush is rather unremarkable seen from afar. Come late September, they begin to stick out conspicuously in fiery regalia, and it's easy to appreciate their ornamental popularity.

They also take hold readily. A small shoot can simply be recklessly placed in any hole, in shade or sun, and it will likely thrive. Given only a few years and a little pruning, even the most singular transplant can be transformed into an ornamental bush.

There are curiosities in the coloring. On the north side of our barn, I planted two specimens roughly eight years ago. They are both thriving bushes of approximately 5 feet high, full and shapely. As far as I can tell, they are the same species, and they receive the same light, water and such. One, without exception, turns fiery red in early September, while its twin remains aloof in its deep greet coat. It always follows in early to mid October, once the first real hard frosts have set in. I can't explain it, which is fine that way by me.

September 27

Six juvenile delinquents descended into the large boughs of the white pines that border the house on the northern side. You'd think from the fanfare that they expected we missed them. Early summer, we experienced the calls of the songbirds, melodious mating songs which began well before dawn and continued throughout the day. Later in the summer they waned, but the background noise of mourning dove and chick-a-dee, evening cardinal and catbird all persisted.

Now there is much less consistency, which made the blue jay cacophony so contrasting. From wherever they resided this summer, it appears these troublemakers have returned, like a gathering of teenagers just wanting to push the boundaries of propriety.

I suppose we'll break out the shelled peanuts soon, tossing them on the back porch in the morning as some sort of appeasement.

September 28

Autumn reminds us that the night sky, with humidity that has lowered since the sultry days of August, shows the heavens in such clarity that it is easy to fall in love with simply gazing at the stars.

The moon is waning enough now to afford more darkness, and the stars appear slowly just after 7:00 pm, with Venus first to arrive. She is brilliant as the evening star, hanging perhaps 15 degrees high on the western horizon after sunset and staying just long enough before dipping below the treelike.

If the lights of Anna Maria are off, it's worth standing on the cross knoll when darkness sets in, particularly if the winds are calm. It Is simply beautiful to scan the horizon, watching for shooting stars and waiting to see if the milky way will resolve.

September 29

Mornings are equally beautiful, in the stillness of the pre-dawn when the sky is clear.

Orion is well overhead nearly, perhaps 10 degrees below meridian at 4:00 in the morning, sitting upward in the southern sky. It's so dark now, that the Orion nebula appears within his sword, barely a fuzzy patch of white against the coal black background.

Jupiter continues to progress ever counter-clockwise, retrograde notwithstanding. It has moved closer to the twins and will reside nearby for the next year. This patch of sky is beautiful now, with Sirius and Jupiter, Orion and Aldeberan, the Hyades and the Pleides all so close together.

September 30

It is fitting that the new moon comes when September is at an end. The changes are undeniable now, much as we would prefer to keep these warm and clear New England days forever. We have been blessed with two weeks of sun-filled days, of blue skies the color of cobalt, where the most distant peaks of Wachusett are clear to see in the dry air. Equally so the night sky has been a wonder of stars, cooler now, where the crickets that remain have begun to struggle in their cadence.

It's too easy to use the struggle analogy this time of year, when there's sign enough that nature is increasingly content with letting go. But these signs need not be solely thought of in terms of decay or endings; there is magnificence in this transition as much as there is decline.

Take our white pines out front as an example. They, like many throughout the town are becoming beautifully two-toned now. A misconception is that pines don't lose their needles like the deciduous trees; the vibrant sugar maples that will soon typify this fact. The truth is that most conifers do thin this time of year, particularly when the late summer and early autumn have been in drought. Just now our white pines are showing brown needles, and it is the case that such pines often drop 1/3 of their needles each year. It is partly to lessen water loss, now that photosynthesis has diminished and partly to simply account for senescence.

The result is a pleasing two-tone of greens and browns among the boughs, whereupon soon enough the ground beneath will gather another carpet layer of soft brown needles once they fall.

October

October 1

There are far more yellow hues in the woods and roadsides now, making the filtered sunlight appear warmer somehow. The climb up South Road from the reservoir is particularly beautiful, where the trees canopy the street just before it intersects Route 31. In summer, the deep greens of oaks and maples and ash created a darkened tunnel that was a welcome cool spot from the summer swelter. Now the same leaves have lost some of their reflected deep greens, and their slow deterioration permits light enough to pass through, giving each a measure of translucence. Driving up the road is simply warmer now, less about the temperature which has given way to cooler autumn and more of perception, where the diffuse yellow is enveloping.

All around town the delicate leaves are just starting to fall to the ground. The birch especially seem ready to retire, having spent several months tirelessly waving in even the most gentle breeze. They are often among the first to yellow and drop, in groups they give way in the autumn wind falling like giant snow flakes to the ground, continuing their carefree waving as they descend, until they come to rest as a golden carpet waiting to be scattered by the passing cars.

October 2

Look for the fuzzy white body of the Hickory Tussock Moth caterpillar. This year, they seem to turn up in all sorts of places. As I write this, one is fast approaching on the driveway, its white body easily visible on the asphalt, undulating as it makes its way.

It's curious where this little thing is intent on going, as it seems to be making a bee-line toward the house. When turned around with a stick, it reorients to the same direction and steadfastly marches onward. I wonder if it is simply going uphill or is following an easterly path, keeping the sun to its right as it goes along.

They are pretty little things, with a black stripe down their midline and tufts of antennae-like black hairs at either end. These are barbed with inflammatory defense, and like our ubiquitous poison ivy, may cause a nasty response to persons who handle the caterpillar.

The adult moth emerges in the spring from a cocoon that has overwintered in the leaf mold. The moth is pale yellow with mottled brown spots and feeds on hickory, ash and oak, among other deciduous fare. With our big blacks out front, it's no wonder we have the caterpillars around in such numbers. They are in the lawn, on windowsills, and in the barn.

October 3

There are many colors at the farm right now, in some ways mirroring what will be the norm around town for a brief period when the leaves turn in earnest.

The fall harvest in full is something to admire, and the store is well stocked with provender that draws from the late summer fare to the autumn root vegetables.

Apple varieties line the window shelves – macs, honey crisps, goldens, pink ladies and Cortlands, each unique in shading and flavor. Next to them reside the plums and peaches, the latter nearly past season, but sweet enough yet to remind the taste buds that summer wasn't too long ago.

The center is filled with egg plant, peppers and squash, and it is nice to simply browse each bin to admire the deep colors of purple and red and yellow. Soon enough, Sarah will make butternut squash soup, hinted with curry and wonderfully delicious, and when we eat it for dinner the smell and flavor simply represents autumn. This is true of cider, which sits on the counter in full and half gallon jugs.

There are still ears of corn and fresh lettuce and tomatoes, but it is becoming more difficult to give them priority. It is October after all, and we have to bid farewell to the summer pleasures sooner or later.

October 4

For a couple of weeks, the quiet in the house has been interrupted by a steady tock, tock, tock, light yet rhythmic. It had the sound of an old wall clock, steadily keeping time while pendulum and escape click and clack unerringly.

It took a bit of investigating to discover the source, partly because the noise would go on only for a minute or so, then stay silent for a while after. At last we saw the chick-a-dees taking an interest in the gutter that sits below the roofline of the sunroom. Evidently, they have been attracted to the pine seed which had been falling gently and it would seem collecting in all places, including the gutter screen. The tock, tock, tock was simply their way of knocking seed to open it, and it reverberated through the house.

Chick-a-dees on the gutter are one thing. Today, the noise was decidedly louder, and we've come to anticipate this problem each early fall. The downy woodpeckers seem to think our wood slat siding and cedar shake are enticing sites for meals. The downy will hammer forcefully, unfortunately making holes in the siding, which necessitates action on our part. Shiny pie pans and toy whirly fans hung from nails placed in spots on the house side seem to work well, driving the pesky downy away, either out of fear or embarrassment.

October 5

The notable climbers are conspicuous now, as their chlorophyll degrades with the waning light and cooler temperatures. The deep greens that served to camouflage them within the pines have faded, such that brilliant reds or yellows cast their presence in sharp relief.

In our front, an enviable poison ivy ascends one of the tall pines, unnoticed really for the past several months. Now, it is a scarlet like no other, rising upward close to the trunk in a way that makes the tree look as if it has caught fire from a distance. All the poison ivy plants have been changing, though the ground variety seem to go to yellow more than anything else. I've noticed that the climbers often tend to red, and I wonder if a difference in variety is to account.

Bittersweet leaves are also rapidly changing to yellow, and they too reveal their presence against the green background. Bittersweet seems to be in all places and mostly unwanted, beautiful in leaf color and later in berry but invasively choking all the while.

Notes:
Towhees still at feeder.
Cricket 57 chirps / minute at thermometer of 50 degrees

October 6

Maples too are increasingly brilliant. Several of the younger sugars down by the library are almost a cardinal red, and when the direct sun hits the leaves it is nearly overwhelming. Many yards throughout town have maples that curiously tend to two tone, with the periphery of the crown turning to color while the lower portions remain a late summer green. I suppose the botanist would explain it on account of lowered sugar production (or pressure) to the outside, or perhaps the effect of slightly lower temperature on the exposed areas. It looks simply as if these majestic trees were secretly removed and their top dunked in red paint, like an ice cream scoop that is given a dressing of hot chocolate that cools hard on the top.

Our big sugar maple next to the sunroom is holding out, still mostly green but certainly tired looking all the same. It tends to yellow uniformly and somewhat late, then drop its leaves nearly as a whole when the first wind-driven rainy day comes.

October 7

A gold finch must have hit the sunroom window this morning, for it sat stunned on the porch, making no effort to flee when I stepped out to investigate. The poor thing was soaking wet from a cold misty rain, its mottled yellow feathers wet through against its body. These same feathers were a brilliant yellow only a few weeks ago, but like the successional change of the deciduous trees, the colors were fading to their more drab winter coat.

Sarah and I lined a small box with tissue, picked up the little bird and placed it inside, taking both to the garage where I had set up a can light to shine within for warmth.

We watched it for twenty minutes as it lay stunned, with beak opening and closing rhythmically, eyes tiny black blinking slowly. All of a sudden, it moved quickly, spreading its wings as if to escape, only to follow with one sudden shudder. Its eyes closed, and it went still, and we both cried at the failure of our effort.

October 8

Wind brought down many of the white pine needles that only yesterday were still on the trees, brown ones whose time had come. The pines all had a two-tone appearance of green and brown, and now they are restored. The ground however is littered with needles, as is the roadway, so many so that entire stretches of pavement are nearly covered. In places where the car tires pass over, the tracks clear the road enough that from a distance it looks like a sandy road, where only this morning it was clear.

These will scatter about and eventually disappear, much like the light snow that falls spindrift on cold pavement, where slight breezes cause it to shift and eddy until warmth erases it entirely.

October 9

The blue jays have been more active these past several days, and soon apart from our cardinal pairs that remain throughout the winter, the jays will be the principal splash of color among our dooryard bird visitors.

Blackbirds are also moving about now; they frequent the fields across the road during the day and call out to one another. I am reminded of the old motto:

By the first of March, the crows begin to search
By the first of April, they are sitting still
By the first of May they are flown away
Creeping greedy back again with October wind and rain.

October 10

There is less visible grass beneath the big maple by the feeders, replaced by a patchwork carpet of yellow and brown leaves which have been the first to come down. It is this same way around town; we are at the peak of color now, maybe even a little past, though only the first wave of leaf fall has started to happen. In most lawns anyway, it is just below the trees that the grass is covered.

Look up, however, and it's plain to see that the vast majority has yet to fall. Out lower woods is still fairly closed in, though peaks of branches and trunks are starting to appear in the distance as thinning in starting to occur.

The woods have taken on a golden tone, and it is simply beautiful. Gold and yellow now predominate, with the fiery reds of climbing vines and burning bushes slowly receding. The viburnams are starting to turn, and perhaps if the conditions are right they will display the purple-red colors before giving way to the frosts that are coming closer.

October 11

The temperature fell twenty degrees overnight with the onset of a cold front that arrived having little fanfare. The morning thermometer registered 38 degrees, and it was deathly quiet in the pre-dawn, save for the sound of distant cars driving on Route 31.

The drive to Holden was particularly striking, in the low valley out of Paxton where the causeway divides the Kendall Reservoir. On both sides, the water surface had wispy tendrils of rising vapor, so much so that the lakes looked ghostly alive with thousands of spectral shapes which moved about slowly in the gentle breeze there.

These shapes were so dense that their numbers obscured the far side spillway house to the south, its stone structure hidden on the opposite shore.

As the road ascended from the causeway up toward Holden, there was a peculiar line of low fog, no thicker than several feet and just at the level of the windshield. In an instant the car climbed through the layer and emerged higher on, and in the rearview mirror the valley became hidden altogether.

October 12

Throughout town, people are continuing to decorate for the fall season; there are corn stalks and gourds and pumpkins on doorsteps.

My guess is that the majority came from the farm here, with this past August and September nearly ideal for growing such crop. Each day we see the grey truck go back and forth to Echo farm multiple times, whether it be to pick up pumpkins or corn, both of which grow in the fields there.

It is unusual this time of year – still picking corn this late in the season, when normally the killing frost would have ended things well enough. It has been strangely warm, making corn on the cob out of place for October. We haven't eaten any since September anyway, as there is a season for everything.

Just now, the driveway in front of the store has jumbles of pumpkins placed on wooden pallets, the piles arranged broadly by size. There are white pumpkins mixed within the mostly orange regulars, and these appear ghostly at night when carved and lit by candle from within.

October 13

At midday a flock of Canada Geese flew overhead. We heard them a half minute or so before seeing them, from the direction of the lower woods northeast of the house. The stillness of the day was broken only by their strident calls from high up.

I counted 22 birds descending in a loose "v," flying over the top of the spruce line before making a wide arc around the fields. Once, twice, they circled, then changed course to land just to the south in the area of the old flats, now given over to a parking lot and grassy area next to the college.

The geese will be seen increasingly now, and once the first real killing frosts arrive they'll likely take to the fields, less worried about tractors or farmers to interrupt their autumn grazing.

October 14

The big buckeye tree in front of the school has been dropping its large seeds for a couple of weeks. I walked down this afternoon with a small backpack to gather a few dozen to keep, mostly just an excuse to take a stroll in town on such a fine October day.

Most of the seed has fallen, and they are largely split – the inner nut having been separated from the outer husk. The latter gets your attention – about the size of a golf ball, with rather nasty spikes all around it. A curious thing really, designed perhaps to protect the inner nut from scavengers like squirrels? But if so, why are most split upon the ground, easily allowing any predators access to the nut. Perhaps the spikes help to break apart any leaf mold or humus or soil, thereby giving the nut a better chance to find purchase until next spring.

The nut itself is quite pretty, the color of darkened wood that has been heavily varnished, save for the singular light spot which conspicuously marks the buckeye all its own.

October 15

Today was another perfect day for simply going anywhere to appreciate the best of this season. The temperature rose to 60 degrees, and there was no wind or clouds at all, giving the sky a nearly cerulean blue color.

The trails of Moore State Park are now covered in leaf fall, and they crunch beneath your feet when you walk, yellow maple leaves, brown oaks, mottled specimens of hickory, ash and beech. The air is tinged with the smell of tannins, and though the majority of leaves have yet to fall, there is thinning of the canopy so that sunlight now enters throughout, creating a warm glow to the woods.

The Old Brigham Road is especially nice, again with leaf fall enough to cover the way. The road here is long abandoned, lined with mountain laurel on both sides, still deep green as if indifferent to the changing of the seasons.

October 16

Rain came last evening, and today was a cool drizzly affair so unlike the past two days. This weather necessitated the woodstove, which has sat fallow since last spring.

The first fires in the stove are pleasant ones, strangely nostalgic for some reason, as if we've forgotten the routine, the mess, and chore of hauling wood, cleaning ash, and maintaining the fire. After months of successively working the stove, by April we have had enough. Now it is delightful, and with plenty of wood in the barn why not fire the stove to ward off the October chill?

An hour after it's been going and the room is finally starting to warm. The dogs seem to have settled right back to their routine of last winter, both lying on their sides not two feet from the hearth. Their fur is nearly hot to the touch, yet they seem perfectly at bliss. It isn't long before the cat joins them, and for awhile all three are content to put aside any differences for the sake of such heat this October day.

October 17

The field next to Anna Maria's cross is filled now with mustard all in bloom. It has been so for a couple of weeks, and when seen from the road the yellows of the blossoms are concentrated so that it is just striking. This same field was sweet corn not two months ago, and when played out the tractor came to turn it under. Evidently within the soil, seeds of last year's mustard lay waiting for just the moment to begin, and the results now show – mustard everywhere. It is not uniform, of course. There are plenty of other perennial weeds throughout, but most are either diminutive or simply not showy that they deserve no special attention.

On the hill top, Fred left a section planted to cabbage, and there are dozens of small butterflies about, yellow and white seeming to travel haphazardly around the field. Again, see from the road the butterflies too look numerous, and the effect of fallow brown rows interspersed with mustard plants all green against the distant hills, where the sky above is the deep autumn blue – it is an idyllic scene.

When it is quiet at these times, when there are no distracting sounds of cars or people, save for the background work of the farm, it is simply beautiful here.

October 18

Hunter moon

The Native Americans proclaimed this full moon as the Hunter Moon, and I suppose it was a time associated with gathering game both large and small to secure provisions of both flesh and fur for the long winter months ahead.

This is the downside of course to later October, as the colors begin to diminish and the trees increasingly become bare. The brilliance of autumn's change is now giving way to our realization that we must prepare both physically and spiritually for the next season.

The autumn of the year is much like the autumn of our own lives, where the harvest that resulted from our productive days has largely been accumulated and set aside. The youthful days of spring's pace, of growth and sensations and vigor have become sweet memories. So too the maturity of our summer, where the drive to grow slackened into our need to provide for the next cycle, and autumn has seen witness to these efforts, resplendent with a renewal of color and vitality that for a moment transports us back to youth.

But this season, like the years, progresses ever onward.

But though there is now a decline in color and in life, there is also something we will come to appreciate as the next few weeks unfold. The passing of the leaves of this year may mark the end of life's production, yet their departure restores vistas to the far hills, hidden for so long by the lower woods that gave so much to our summers. We now have clarity and distance in vision to the hills beyond and perhaps more understanding of its value in the scheme of the cycle of the seasons.

October 19

The big maple next to the feeders by the sunroom is losing its leaves quickly now, and in today's breeze they've fallen like large snowflakes from the sky.

Within an hour's time, the ground beneath has become littered as a mosaic of differing shades of yellow, and the larger branches are now visible, where the past several months they've been hidden. Tomorrow morning when I turn on the spotlight to check for raccoons or skunks, I expect it will be more illuminated here, where the light reflects off the fallen leaves. It's much the same in winter, where our snow covered ground is notably more bright, of course.

It is pleasant to walk through the layer now, shuffling my feet so that the crisp leaves make their familiar noise, and a small trail of grass shows through in my foot's wake.

October 20

A cold front came in last evening, and with it a harsh autumn breeze that spoke of changes ahead. In the hour before dawn, the newly gibbous moon cast the woods in shadows as blackened trunks, and upper branches became more visible, where only yesterday they were hidden in foliage.

Just now, the wind is steady, and it is raining leaves all around, opening more vista with each passing minute.

October 21

Roughly ten years ago, the town planted hybrid versions of the Great American Chestnut, the once mighty giant which had been decimated by the blight in the mid twentieth century. Nearly fifty seedlings were placed in a protective area of Moore State Park, cordoned off and allowed to grow.

Three weeks ago I made a point of checking the trees, for I recall last year that several showed signs of producing nut casings after ten years of growth. The seedlings had matured to nearly 25-foot tall adolescents, and had reached the point of reproduction.

Today I returned to discover that certain individuals had created and dropped their nut casings, which now lay strewn about on the ground, opened from having dried in the sun and causing the nuts to have jostled loose.

The casings of chestnuts are formidable in appearance and in design. They are notably spiked, resembling the spiny shell of a sea urchin and roughly the same size. The spines are dangerously prickly and difficult to even hold gingerly in your hand. Each casing is designed to house 3 chestnuts, and these are similar in appearance to the buckeye nut, medium brown with an oval patch that is faded at the point where it connects to the casing. They are more kernel shaped than the buckeye and similarly hard shelled.

I gathered roughly thirty nuts and brought them home. American Chestnuts, ready for me to try roasting just as the familiar song from my youth were Nat King Cole tells of roasting on the open fire.

I slit the end of each nut, placed them in the oven for 15 minutes, and allowed them to cool just enough to safely handle, then quickly pealed the outer hard shell to reveal the pale yellow meat within.

They tasted like a sweetened potato, with a similar texture - warm and Earthy in a way.

October 22

The old Snow House a quarter of a mile up Grove Street from 122 stands out notably in the October sky. For the past several years, the house has been painted an ochre-colored yellow, matching nicely to the autumn-tinged leaves of the large maples that sit on the hillside beneath. It is doubtful that this present color is authentic, which would have likely been shakes or white clapboard, but altogether it looks appropriate just now.

The house is over 250 years old, and I imagine this area as sparse farm land, where Grove was nothing more than a dirt road or two-track that connected from Leicester, making its way down toward what is now the Pine Hill Reservoir. This water is recent really, where the construction of the dam created the reservoir and submerged the old road that connected Grove toward Rutland.

The Snow House is purported to have its own resident ghost, and occupants have reported various poltergeist activities for generations. How fitting for an October season that progresses onward toward our Halloween.

October 23

A northwest wind picks up the leaf fall in the yard, swirling about the dry oak and cherry cast offs and making little dust devil-looking figures. These settle into small piles that lay still until another gust animates them this way and that.

The front portion of the barn has leaves piled against the foundation, having come to rest there from an eddy where the wind tunnels between an adjacent white pine and the corner of the barn. These leaves are two feet deep, covering the foundation like a protective blanket.

I've read that such shoring up of foundations was the norm a hundred years ago. Families would gather the leaf fall and grasses and pile them up all around the foundation of the house, even using fencing to retain the material as insulation. This barrier would help protect the house from winter's draft, at a time when home foundations weren't so overly sealed from the external environment.

October 24

Out of the corner of my eye, I caught sight of a vole that had wandered into the roadway near the break line of woods just uphill from the Cheney Farm. The morning was yet dark, and the movement was highlighted by the yellow streetlight that shone downward onto the road. A tiny thing, maybe just smaller than a field mouse, but it scurried with such a frenzy, first weaving outward into Grove and then returning to the curbside. It was trapped here, not able to negotiate the curb height, and so it resigned to frantic movement up the roadside. I half expected an owl to swoop down for an easy catch.

We don't often see the voles, save for the presence of their winter tunnels that form near the surface pack and curiously in the proximity of the feeder. Their coat reminds me of the velvety brown of a domesticated rabbit, and I am curious if it feels the same.

October 25

Yesterday's vole is a reminder that the house will soon start to receive its late fall occupants. With the onset of cold nights, the barn nests are becoming less comfortable, and the field mice (or deer mice) will seek warmer quarters for the winter. I suspect that soon we will hear the scurrying of tiny feet in the wall passages of our old home. We've come to accept these autumnal intruders as simply a normal part of the seasonal transition.

Old homes are usually inhabited by all manner of creatures, great and small. The foundations and sills possess the inevitable cracks and holes which provide access to the mice who seek shelter.

This transition will also mean that the cat will be back in business, as the transient mice sometimes wander into the basement. It is always in the middle of the night when we hear the scuffle in the basement and the squeaks of protest when the mice are caught and tossed about.

In mast years, when either the food source has been abundant for the mice, or when the predators have been low, the cat is kept rather busy for the initial months of November and December. We once kept a tally of caught mice, the number having reached in the lower 20s by the time the holidays arrived.

Friends who live in contemporary homes are horrified when they learn of our late autumn tenants. Such is the way of modernity, when newly constructed dwellings are sealed nearly air tight, shutting off the occupants from such surprises.

October 26

The remaining maple leaves in the yard, left unattended after having escaped our raking two days ago, have faded from their golden yellow to a light brown. This morning they are curling on the edges, where the touch of frost from the last evening has collected on the veins, making each leaf appear highlighted in dusty-white sparkles.

The grass is also tinged in white, crunching beneath our feet as we walk and leaving footprint depressions that strangely melt in the wake of passing. These remain as darkened prints against the frosted lawn, waiting until the morning sun warms enough to erase the effect.

These frosts ebb and flow now, creeping in steadily in the night and staying longer in the morning with each passing day. Soon they will take hold for the long stretch, were the radiant warmth is too feeble to stem the tide of winter's approach.

October 27

The thin white toothed asters have gone to seed head within the past few days. There are places along the road where only a month ago the white petals dominated so, that it was easy to imagine the ditches were covered in a sparse dusting of snow. Now there are tiny puff balls of seeds, each like small dandelion heads clustered among the browning foliage that was green only yesterday, it seems.

Take a stick and
quickly swing through
a grouping of them,
and watch as hundreds
of blowies take to the
air, bound for
wherever the wind
disperses them. It looks
like a miniature snow
globe, where the seeds
flit about in the light
breeze then settle in
layers one on top
another upon the
ground.

The milkweed pods too
have dried and opened, spilling forth thousands of
seeds which simply await the wind to carry them

aloft. There is a large grouping near the north stone wall of the arm, with pods that dangle open and clusters of silken seeds ready. Many have simply fallen to the ground below in clumps of white brought down by the weight of the misty rain two days ago.

Those that remain cling yet to the pod husk, drying in the frosted morning and awaiting the building breeze which will carry them skyward.

October 28

As the leaf colors fade and fall to collect in the yards and roadways about town, the sere browns of tall grass and corn stubble stand out in the field. Lawns have begun to go dormant, bordered by woods where the dark vibrancy of summer has given way to bare branches and sunlight that filters to the ground. October's brilliance is changing to November's muted tones.

There are still outliers in the woods: A maple that holds on to its golden leaves for no apparent reason when all around it have seen the change. Some lawns in town are yet inexplicably green, bordered by burning bush or viburnum that hold tightly to their auburn coat. Soon though, the predominant tones will be shades of brown and yellow and faded greens, amid Earthy scents of tannin which is broken by the fleeting odor of wood smoke from down the road. This will persist until the freeze takes hold, and then we will start to lose even our autumnal scents and colors as the snow approaches.

October 29

Not all is increasingly drab, despite my tone of yesterday. There are still striking colors amid the browns and faded greens, and these mid-autumn treasures remind us that there is yet beauty even as there is decline.

The bittersweet vines are losing their leaves, but the berries stand out nicely, making random patterns in the bushes that they climb or trailing shapes like beads on a string that wind up the tree trunks. The berry shells are starting to split, opening to reveal the bright red fleshy fruit within. They will remain this way for some time, and the drabness of the bare trees are offset by the pretty two-tone of the bittersweet strands.

Look now to moist lowlands to see winterberry. It is nearly impossible to overlook the bright red fruits, set in clumps close to the deep green of the bush, with leaves slightly oval and waxy, much in the appearance of holly. The berries are ripening now and will provide provender for the late autumn birds.

There is a spectacular group of winterberry now down by the roadside bog past Robinson's. The greens of the wetland here have mostly faded, making the bush all the more outstanding.

October 30

The first hard frost arrived overnight, showing itself
in the coming light of dawn with tomato and pepper
leaves now curled and burned looking. The ground
around is feathery white and crunches beneath the
boot, dog's paws also shuffling with crackling noises
amid frozen leaf fall and autumn grass which are
highlighted in white.

As the dogs pad onward, little puffs of steam are
visible from their nose and mouth with each outward
breath, and they remind me of small steam engines
giving off white clouds as they move ahead.

The hard frost is late this year, but it has arrived
nonetheless, and now the growing season is officially
at an end. So too are the hordes of insects, so evident
only a few weeks ago as background noises of all
sorts; now there is only silence in the morning. It is
unsettling after so much life, and we must grow
accustomed again to this phase of quiet, awaiting the
long stretch that allows all life to recharge and renew.

October 31

October at an end, and many signs point to the
transition to early winter.

The chipmunks have been busy on the back porch,
and it is amusing to watch them at work. One sits in
an old toy wagon we keep near the feeders, where

Sarah casts a handful of seed each morning after filling the tubes. During the summer, the ground feeding birds and gray squirrels would jump into the wagon to retrieve the easy pickings.

Now the chipmunks are monopolizing the pile, knowing it as an easy source for their winter granaries. They hop gingerly into the small wagon bed and stuff their pouches full, stopping every so often to raise their head and look about for signs of trouble before resuming their work.

It's a wonder they don't tip forward when they leave the porch, bound for dens somewhere in the yard, mouth bulging on both sides from the gluttony of gathering. They are simply endearing to watch, and we know that soon they will enter their holes for good, until spring.

November

November 1

A driving rain came last evening and spoiled things for the trick-or-treaters, though at least it was a warm front where temperatures rose through the night.

By morning, the light revealed that the remaining leaves had come down with the deluge, and the gloomy start cast everything in a muted fog. In the large puddles in the driveway, leaves floated on the surface, spinning slowly about in the wind.

November it seems wants to arrive all of a sudden, stealing the last of autumn's colors from the limbs and dashing them about on the ground. The only consolation is the strangely warm wind, which is reminiscent of an April front, where the Earthy smells percolate and excite us toward spring.

November 2

It is closing day this Saturday at the farm, and though there will be a trickle of last minute customers for the next week or so, the activity will notably slow. With the late front in October, it's been a long growing season, yet it is remarkable how quickly it seems to have gone by.

Last week saw the men in the front field nearly all day long, picking leeks by pulling them each out of the black plastic and cleaning the outer layer of skin from the bottom. These were made into groups of three, and such bundles were sold to the foreigners, mostly.

Now the root crops have largely gone, save for several bushels of potatoes, carrots, turnips and such. I suspect it will all go within the next week or so.

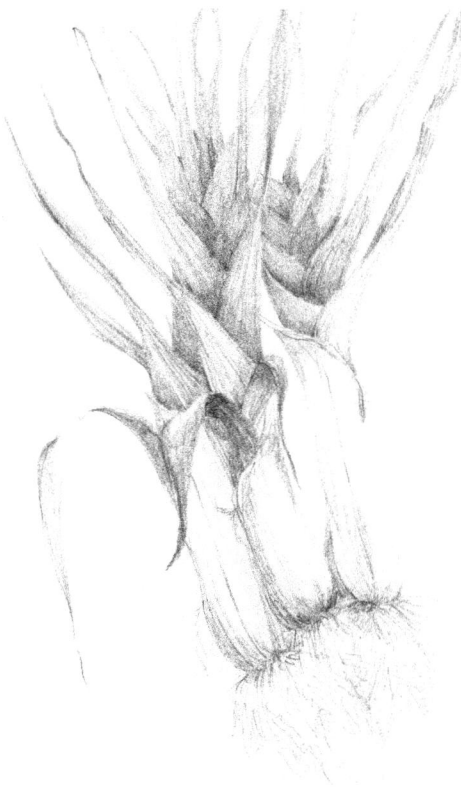

After this, we rely on whatever stores we've made (and of course the grocery) to get us through till next spring. We are already starting to miss the benefit of fresh vegetables.

Opening day was around June 20th, though the work of seeding, plowing, preparing the beds, and transplanting had begun in early May. This makes six months of demanding work, and I imagine that the fallow time is sorely needed.

November 3

In the afternoon sun, the mustard plants are golden in the harvested field next to the knoll that fronts the Anna Maria cross. While most foliage around has been fading quickly to yellow and brown, taking on the look we expect in November, these Brassicas are as vibrant green as seen in midsummer growth.

No less beautiful are the yellow petals, thousands of them now, set atop the deep greens that for a moment is tempting to imagine them as June dandelions covering a distant field.

Even flitting among them are cabbage white butterflies, several that seem to go about helter skelter from plant to plant. It seems strange to see them now, as we've had a hard frost, but somehow this last generation has survived.

The cabbage whites came first in April and May, then again in July and August. This last cycle persists until late autumn, and we enjoy seeing them until the first series of successive freezes arrive.

November 4

Daylight savings time is upon us, that artificial contrivance of Dr. Franklin to allow, in part, an extension of the working farm day.

Farm chores now have made a transition, and we should soon hear the tractors again now that the store has closed. The fields have remnants of crops unpicked, and these will be turned under to promote their return to the soil.

It is more encouraging to see the plow in May, for it signals the beginning of the growing season, when we are filled with wonder and anticipation of root and shoot, leaf and flower. November plowing is a sign of ending, where vestiges of last summer's production are put back to the Earth.

It is a necessary thing to do – to allow for the organic components of life to cycle back to its constituents, to become part of the fodder that will one day next spring be taken up by new life as the season renews.

The fields won't likely be turned bare this time. We should see shoots of winter rye within the week, the cover crop that will hold the soil and store nutrients for the winter, until spring plowing will return it once again.

November 5

The first snow arrived today, calmly in the morning
as tiny flakes that came with a cold front, half hearted
mostly, as they sparsely fell to the ground.

Dawn is earlier now, with the time change of two
days ago, and this snow happened as the building
light revealed a clearing sky, making the combination
of sparse flakes and filtered sunlight strangely
calming.

This was no winter-like storm, announcing its
prematurity with fierceness. Rather, it is as if the
season is content to gracefully reveal that autumn can
be gently succeeded by the coming of winter.

November 6

The temperature dropped to the low 20s overnight,
and by morning the thermometer read 18 degrees.

In the driveway, low spots in the asphalt still held
small pools of water from an overnight rain of two
nights ago, yet these had frozen since last evening.
Their surface now revealed crystalline patterns,
designs of ice that resembled feathery marks, some
that extended for a foot or more.

As the sunrise came, a slight breeze grew gently,
stirring the remaining leaves on those trees which
autumn had yet to claim. These are the strange
outliers about town – the silver maples that line the

roadside, with yet full foliage of yellow leaves when all about them have fallen. So too the crab apples and beech, those few we see in yards or fields that inexplicably hang on.

In the warming light, the wind in their boughs causes the leave to fall quickly today, and it is strange to see them dropping nearly as one, when only a whisper of breeze affects in the golden sunlight of morning.

I read once that such trees held bits of moisture in each of the new buds that lay just underneath where the petiole connects the old leaf to the stipule of the branch. In hard frosts, the moisture freezes and expands, breaking the hold of the petiole, though keeping it affixed in the grips of the hardened water. As the tree is warmed in the morning sunshine, the moisture melts enough that the gentle breeze causes all to release and drop to the ground, a shower of late fall color.

November 7

They were pulling up the plastic row bedding across the street today. A stiff breeze from the south helped lift the edges, sending the released length of black billowing into the air, bits of fastened soil and plant material splaying in all directions.

Beneath lay the rounded rows of dark moist soil, interspersed with the remnant stalks of harvested plants. For a moment, we thought of the spring, when these rows were newly made, and the soil was richly brown and unmolested with weeds.

Between the rows is another thing altogether, filled with a mixture of drying ragweed, lamb's quarters, shepherd's purse, and pigweed – the summer annuals that all compete for this field, this light, soil and nutrients. Pepperweed and mustard also thrive, yet the recent frosts have taken their toll.

A few remain unaffected, seemingly content to grow in this late season. In the two-track edges there is henbit flourishing, low to the ground, with terminal leaves that bear small, purple flowers that resemble miniature snap dragons. These henbits are of the mint family, though their leaves offer to associative odor when crushed.

November 8

The young deer have been active these past two weeks, and we see them in the early morning or in the evening, walking through the woods next to the house either coming from or going to the fields.

The changing daylight has hastened the rut, causing young bucks to lose their senses in pursuit of the does, who are now in estrus. The result is that we must be cautious – the deer are more reckless in the roadway, and when driving we look to the woods that border Grove Street, scanning for the reflection of deer eyes in the headlights.

Hunters too will be in the woods, for it is bow season and this means that we wear bright colors for awhile, particularly in the woods.

November 9

In the valley where Marshall Street descends on its way toward Kettlebrook Farm, the creek that passes underneath the road is frozen over.

Though we've had a dry autumn, the water here is still surprisingly wide, perhaps eight feet across where it pools in a small basin before entering the culvert.

Now there is a fair skim across the expanse, and the winding creek is also frozen up the feeder slope, interrupted here and there by sere grasses that poke upward through the ice.

Beyond the bend, where the water follows downhill to this basin, it must still be unfrozen; the flow is likely made turbulent where it strikes the edge of the ice, moving underneath the skim and bringing air bubbles along.

Standing on the roadside I watch the air moving beneath, thinking that it resembles quicksilver trickling along the dark expanse.

November 10

November seems unforgiving with sunshine, where
steel gray skies and low ceiling clouds predominate
more often than not. When the bright rays do appear,
set now at a low angle and diffusely yellow on even
the most clear day, they reveal a woods which is
largely brown, save for the evergreens here and there.

November can be a bleak transition from the splendor
of October till the crisp and clean snows of December
arrive.

November 11

A strong wind blew the entire day, cold and forceful
as the late autumn gales tend. It seems crueler now,
when the gray skies and bare branches are the
primary sign of the season's change. This breeze in
January will be biting, which is harsh in its own way,
but such a wind in November is colder still; our
temperature is 39 and the air is moist, making this
day as raw as can be.

The spruce line across the road released their small
cones, shaken loose no doubt by the tempest, leaving
the yard and driveway on the lee side a mess with
hundreds of them.

I brought a handful inside and set them on the mantle
above the woodstove, where they spent the better
part of the afternoon and evening drying in the warm
spot above the box. At some point in the night, the

cones relaxed and spilled several small winged seeds, miniature versions of the maple keys we see falling from the sky.

November 12

At first light the rain began to change over to snow, falling first as large white clumps, laden with moisture and dropping quickly to the ground. Within fifteen minutes the front began to arrive, picking up the wind and causing the temperature to drop a little. The flakes responded, becoming smaller and more numerous, and they fell at an angle in the building breeze.

Soon, the back porch was coated with a white layer, as was the grassy area around the bird feeders in the side yard, save for the paving stones that form a rough path from the porch door to the berm. These remained wet, still holding the latent heat of the Earth to melt the falling snow.

Only the lee side of the trees had grassy areas that were uncovered by snow, and from the sun porch window looking outward in the gloaming morning light, these green patches that matched the trunks looked like shadows cast upon the snowy ground.

November 13

Viburnams about the town are now rapidly changing. They are among the last of the deciduous plants to lose their leaves, it seems, and the recent cold has only hastened the change.

They are remarkable really, beautiful and varied from spring till now. The early leaves in May came easily enough, lime green and small versions of the mature form which resulted. This was curious to watch, as the leaves seemed to arrest at a medium size in June, only to grow slowly beyond into the early autumn. I recall seeing ours out front and thinking it to be thin looking in early summer. Now, its leaf cover is full, not so much by the addition of new ones as much as the continued growth of those that formed so early. They are dropping now, making the bush appear thin again.

These leaves are mottled, no two alike and range from purple to brown, yellow to red. The effect is a rich mosaic, so autumn like in appearance. As they fall, the ground beneath takes on a blanket which contrasts well with the remaining then snow cover of yesterday.

November 14

The big oaks in front catch the morning sunlight on their southern face, warming the bark on this cold morning for an hour or so until the angle shifts enough so that they are cast in shadow.

Up close, their bark is deeply furrowed and patchy with bits of deep green moss that looks like miniature forests seen from above.

Standing nearby with the sun on my back, the absence of wind made it seem warmer than the air temperature, and it was easy to imagine the moss as verdant forests upon some gray landscape seen from high above.

Next to one large group of moss, a lightning beetle sat immobile, its body wedged within a deeper furrow so that the moss canopy partially shielded its carapace. I leaned in and breathed warm air on it, encouraging its antennae to respond in flicking about slowly to the energy-giving warmth.

Several breaths and the beetle began to move slowly away, and whether it was due to the warmth or something other in my breath I don't know.

November 15

The twilight before dawn and again following sunset are both more noticeably shorter than they tranquil pace of summer's gloaming. Now the light comes quickly in the morning, just after the area of sky in the east which marks the approach of the coming day. But this is followed in earnest by the daylight as if the countryside awakens quickly in November to prosper from as much of these miserly days as possible. We are reminded that the sun is up for only 8 ½ hours or so at this point.

November 16

Between the lower field of the farm and the cultivated grounds of Anna Maria, the acre of fallow land has changed notably these past several years. Time was when one of the men would use the tractor and mowing deck to cut back the yearly scrub, leaving this land a shorn breakline between field and college.

It has always been a wet parcel, where the water table rises on bedrock that is close to the soil, such that the spring season finds water percolating here on the surface, flowing down the natural valley. The moist soil promotes all sorts of early successional plants to thrive, and hence necessitates the aggressive mowing.

This has been neglected these past several years, and the field is now replete with sumac trees and tall grasses, the former so dense that it is nearly impossible to walk through.

They are beautiful now, to see them from the two-track that connects the upper to the lower field, hundreds of sumacs, all leafless and skeletal, reaching upward in disarray. Most bear the red candle, faded somewhat from the cardinal flame of a month ago.

Spread within are sere milkweed plants, dozens of them with dried pods that lay open with silken seeds that have spilled forth. When the breeze strikes, several scatter about, lifting among the sumacs and floating upward and beyond to the lower woods.

It is simply beautiful here.

November 17

An unusually warm day, with afternoon sunlight low
in the sky, casting everything in a more golden sheen.
It is remarkable how much the intensity has changed
from only just a month ago, though pleasing all the
same as the landscape takes on a soft, sepia-like feel.

The tractor across the road was out, using tines to
loosen the soil from underneath an unpicked row of
carrots. Strange to hear it now, when the fields have
been nearly buttoned up for the approach of winter.

Sarah and I walked through the spruce line and up
the row to join Larry, who was busy picking carrots
and placing them discriminately into worn bushel
baskets. The best were intended for the food bank,
while the remaining were left rudely behind on the
row surface, food for the deer or to decompose as
next spring arrives.

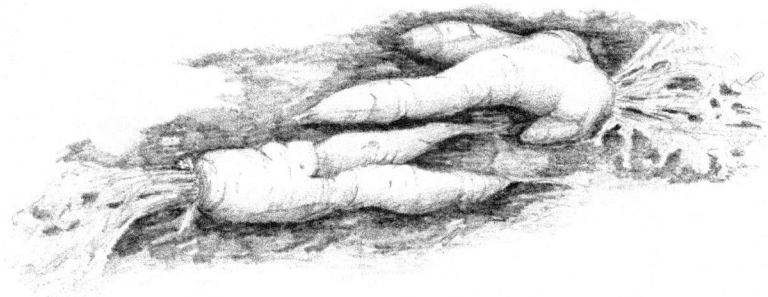

Working the row was a pleasant affair, warm enough
and with no wind that made the job less a chore and
more a chance to simply enjoy working in the soil.
This will end soon enough.

November 18

Hard rain brought down more cones; spruces just across the road now litter the street, some getting caught in the small stream which forms in the shoulder with the heavy rain. They make their way down Grove, some slowing in the small eddies or sandbars of silt. Most only travel a dozen feet or so before coming to rest where the shoulder berms against the roadside.

Across from Sunset Lane there is a large white pine on the old Prentiss property. It too has shaken loose its reluctant cones, brown and closed tightly on the ground. These cones were green last spring, spotted with pitch that smelled of familiar deep woods, waiting to be touched by the clouds of pollen released in May.

Now the cones are dry, and we collect handfuls of them to place by the woodstove. They will open slowly in the dry heat, spilling forth small seeds, and we will use the remnant cones as crackling additions to the going fire.

November 19

The clipping barks began sometime after midnight, from the direction of the lower woods. Having been awakened abruptly by the noise, I decided to go out to the back porch to simply listen.

The nearly full moon was still high so that the back yard and border trees were cast in a silver light, and despite the cold temperature, the lack of wind made it comfortable enough to stand outside.

Another bark-like call, cropped and staccato, followed by several yips, all seemingly just beyond the edge of the treeline at the base of the yard where it abuts the woods. Then I heard a movement – a rustling of leaves down below as if several of the coyotes were gathering.

We go for months without hearing their cries, particularly in the rearing months of summer, when I imagine that any new pups are holed away in forest dens. Come autumn and winter we are reminded of their presence here, like this night, when the eerie bark and longing cries travel clearly in the cold silent forest.

November 20

Coyotes on the move means that all manner of vulnerable creatures are in danger. When we moved to our old house, the neighbors warned us not to let our cats outside for fear of coyotes, fox and even fishers. Since, we've seen them all and have been aware of certain neighbor pets that have gone missing.

Autumn seems to have a way of reminding us of our proximity to the wild and its austerity. At the same time that the environment is becoming harsher, certain animals are more frequent in preparation. Thus we see the bears at the feeder, raiding the supply to put on stores. The coyote and fox are on the move, the former rarely seen though often heard. Fox we do witness, furtively crossing the road in the morning light or brief twilight of evening. It hunts the fields I suspect and travels to and from its woodsy den.

November 21

The Guinea Fowl at the Cheney Farm have nearly reached maturity, and the five birds we see in the morning gather near the roadside fence in the daylight, calling uniquely in alarm when anything out of sorts passes nearby.

Bruce nurtured a half dozen eggs in the incubator last spring and transferred the chicks to a brooding yard after their arrival. Throughout the summer they remained mostly protected and given increasingly free reign to the front barnyard, which itself has always been a jumble of cast-off machinery and assorted implements. We've grown accustomed to all manner of chickens, roosters and turkeys throughout the years, the latter always mysteriously disappearing right around this time of the season. This is just as well, for the birds tend to wander recklessly into Grove, and we have in the past come upon a scene of feathers in the street where some poor bird met its end being struck by a car.

Bruce indicates that this summer has seen more red tail hawks overhead, and a few of the chickens and even a Guinea have become prey. The remainder scatter quickly when a shadow passes overhead, evidently a learned behavior or instinctual response. Now that the ravens have returned for the autumn, the smaller birds are still at risk as are the eggs that have been set within the brooder.

November 22

The pond at Moore State Park is skimmed over with ice, likely having formed a couple of days ago during the cold night in the teens. Even with day temps running in the 40s, it isn't enough to turn back the tide of the coming freeze.

Water still flows freely underneath the bridge that crosses the spillway here. At the edge, there rests the shelf of the now thickening ice, where the flow beneath carries small bubbles and cast off detritus from the growing season. They emerge only for a moment before falling off the precipice and to the holding pond below, waiting in queue to enter the cataract of the mill cascade.

November 23

A gentle front came overnight, bringing a warming rain that ended sometime before daybreak.

In the darkness of the predawn, it was strangely Earthy smelling where the wispy breeze from across the road carried the scent of the turned fields and wet asphalt. For a moment, it was easy to imagine that spring was arriving, with its signs of renewal close at hand.

This is fleeting, we know, and the forecast is for an arctic blast to race in on the heels of this respite, re-freezing the ground more deeply perhaps, to the point that no ephemeral thaw can overturn.

November 24

While the yard is still free of snow, we really should finish the job of raking the last of the leaf fall that now rests sparsely about. The culprits are the black oaks, who hold tenaciously to their sere leaves well after the cast offs of their brilliant neighbors have been tidied to the side of the yard.

It is easy to justify overlooking this chore, now that our enthusiasm for autumn raking has come and gone. We may as well put the rakes in the barn, though to do so necessitates seeing the snow shovels that rest inside the door, and it's difficult to swap one big job in anticipation of another.

The yard around the barn, from the garden down by the lower woods to the back porch is a strange patchwork. Now that the summer crab has died back to yellow and brown, there are sadly few greens to be found, save for the curious islands of thyme which have aggressively established. Sarah grew thyme in a spot near the foundation years ago, and since it has sought fit to spread outward into the yard. In the summer, when I would mow, either my foot on trampling or the blade upon cutting would release the distinct herbal odor, making the area smell vaguely of cooking.

November 25

There are eleven chick-a-dees near the tube feeders this morning, either perched in front of an opening to extract seed or waiting patiently on the crook of the pole for a space to open. The ground beneath is too crowded with the return of the juncos in full measure, where a dozen or so mill about quickly.

An arctic blast of air has increased the activity, where the birds are simply desperate to forage as quickly as possible the moment the gloaming light of morning arrives. I read a study that suggests chick-a-dees will spend nearly the entire waking day on these frigid periods collecting seed, having to consume enough high-energy fare simply to allow them stores to last through the dark stretch of the night. It is the most raw cut of survival we witness where the frenetic pace at the tube provides our own watching pleasure.

When I step outside they rapidly depart to the pines in the berm or in the access border, only to return shortly, alighting on the reaching branches of the maple to measure my intent. It's impossible not to love these gregarious little birds, who give their quizzical squawk and pip with a slightly tilted head and beady black eye. They regard us all with an air of familiarity or recognition before flying down to the feeder again.

November 26

This clipper wind is cutting, and the wind chill is such that even the wood stove can't keep the fireplace room all that warm. The only consolation is the brilliant sky, though it is deceiving with these temps in the low teens.

The trail to the vernal pool near Asnebumskit is leaf covered, and though it passes protectively in a natural hollow so that the winds do not reach, there is the sound of it all in the upper canopy. It is a roaring force that moves the tops of the big trees and makes the distinctive creaking sound when the trees rub together.

The squirrel nests have been more easily visible since the leaves have come down, and now they are conspicuous overhead moving about in the winds. I imagine them tucked neatly inside the darkened nest, comfortably insulated against the cold and wind by layered leaves and bedding, yet it must be a tumultuous affair today.

November 27

There has been no sign of the chipmunks for three days, ever since the arctic front seemed to herald an early winter. Likely they have retreated to their dens to ride out the next season, spending the months in torpor and surviving off the provender in their granaries. There are moments we envy this ability.

These dens must be extensive, and I'm to understand that there are multiple entries about. Evidently there are distinct chambers for sleeping and feeding, eating and rearing, and so I imagine subterranean complexes all about the yard and wood.

It seems only yesterday that the chipmunks would taunt us in the back, perched on the old stone wall that marks the beginning of the access road from the berm. They would "cheep, cheep" loudly, calling to one another, then scurrying in chase, tempting the dogs to pursue them into the hole in the wall.

November 28

We are thankful for the little things on this day, apart from the feelings of security in family, friends, and home. Perhaps above all, we recognize that in the waning of this year, as the darkness settles in for the long haul ahead, we begin to tally the experiences large and small that this year has provided.

These are the things that sustain us through the winter that will be, with the hope and anticipation that we will experience them again as one season of rest gives way to the cycle of renewal.

My own tally of this Paxton year includes:

- The sight of the first yellow crocus, revealed as the snowpack recedes from the garden's edge
- The laughing cry of the pileated, startled by my presence in its woodland home
- The mist that hangs above the wetland on Route 122 near Brooks Road, catching the rising sun and making ghostly shapes
- The lonely cry of the blue heron as it flies alone overhead in the waning light of a still summer evening.
- The smell of the diesel tractor that crests the ridge in the field across the road, dragging a plow that turns the fields to chocolate brown
- The predawn view of Orion in early autumn, seen overhead from Grove Street, framed by the late season trees on either side of the road

- The summer smell of Davis Hill Road after a rain shower, filled with the perfume of sweet grass and milkweed blossom.

November 29

My friend Bill is gathering greenery in the backwoods near his home, in preparation for the holidays that will all too soon be upon us. This is a pleasant tradition – to secure boughs of cedar and arbor vitae, binding them in series, either in a circle as a wreath or as one length to use as garland atop the mantle.

We have a couple of weeks yet before we too trek to the lower woods to search for a suitable Christmas tree. This initial foray will be to locate a few good candidates, and we will then return in another week with a hand saw and truss to pull it out.

Of course we could simply purchase a tree like most tend to do. Even now there are some to be bought in front of the hardware store in Holden, and in another week we will increasingly see evergreens tied down to the rooftops of cars, being transported to homes all about. These are the farm-raised trees, grown just so and shaped for aesthetics, in my mind almost as artificial as the synthetic trees for sale.

Our tree will fall short of these store bought specimens. It will lack by comparison in shape and size, yet I would have it no other way. We locate and cut and haul our own to celebrate the tradition of bringing the living greenery within our home, which is ultimately the connection that we wish in these holy days to come.

November 30

November at an end, and the town trucks were out last night for the first time this season. We heard them lumbering slowly down the road, spreading salt in anticipation of a small storm that was to bring an inch or so of wet snow.

The forecast didn't pan out save for a transitional rain which was more nuisance than anything; we're still in a fair drought from the deficit of this past several months. (The upper reservoir along Route 56 is evidence of this, as the water has depleted so that it is nearly possible to walk across.)

The salted roads were a bluish slurry at daybreak, with small streams of runoff moving down the roadside, taking it all downhill and collecting where we can only imagine with reluctance.

By the afternoon, the sun shone through for a few hours, enough to hasten the evaporation of moisture from the pavement. What remained were the remnant salts not carried to the roadside, leaving the surface chalky white and making it look as if a light dusting of snow happened after all.

December

December 1

The two-track across the road is now frozen, making the going at once easier and more difficult. The sandy soil of each lane is fixed in place so that our boots stay clean where just last week a walk here resulted in clinging mud. The dogs certainly seem to prefer it like this; their paws stay clean after a walk around the fields.

The path is also less forgiving – the differences in freezing have created small ridges and bumps that stay in place where before they would yield to passing boot. Where larger rocks rest in the track, the soil around them has expanded in the freeze, making it look as if the stones have sunk slightly into the Earth.

Where the tractor cut across the path, as it left the corner of the field turned under a week ago, its tread remains fixed in the track. This will continue, fossil like, through snow that piles high with coming storms and winter winds that drift the pack until the ground here is bare. This will endure until the spring thaw, when the warming rains and turning soil work the land toward another planting season.

December 2

Clear and still this morning, so much so that it was easy to hear the bells of the First Congregational Church from the back porch. Six times they chimed, pausing a couple of seconds in between each - strangely the only sound at all outside now.

Six in the morning is very dark in December, made more so by the new moon which officially arrives tomorrow. It seems like just yesterday that mornings were filled with the vibrancy of birdsong or insect; these have been replaced by a December stillness that is so quiet that it's almost lonely.

December 3

The fox may be on the move again, for I've seen them twice now in the same location crossing the road in what must be a corridor. Three mornings ago and again today, in the hours before dawn, a pair emerged from the driveway located next to the wetland area on Route 122 just west of where Grove Street intersects. First came one fox, trotting slowly across the road from the driveway, stopping within the border of trees on the other side that marks the entrance to Crowningshield.

It paused there within for a couple of seconds, then gave a sharp barking call, shrill and intent. A moment later its companion emerged from the same driveway, following the same track across the road and into the woods, presumably both headed for a den somewhere in the small forest that stands between the outlying homes in the development and the first reservoir of the Kettlebrook ponds below.

December 4

The rhododendron throughout town are more conspicuous, in part because their deep green and broad leaves stand distinct against the background of stems and branches, the neighboring trees and bushes whose leaves have fallen away. It is almost as if the rhododendron is indifferent to the change of seasons, carrying on much as it has done since we first took notice of it last spring, when the purple, pink and white blossoms were nearly overwhelming.

The buds that will become next spring's flowers sit idly now, fattened just slightly and a pale tan, waiting until warming conditions spur them to mature.

All is not quiet however, and here is where the rhododendron is curious. In the warming day, when temperatures run above approximately 35 degrees, the leaves are full and positioned nearly perpendicular to the stem. At freezing they begin to noticeably droop, and when the thermometer falls below 25 degrees the leaves curl closed. Colder yet and the curl tightens, concentrating the green color into drooping cylinders that appear lifeless.

Early mornings this time of year find them tightly formed, yet as the day progresses and the feeble sun helps modestly to push the air above freezing, the plant responds – opening leaves slowly and causing them to extend.

Why they do this isn't really as important as is the wonder that they do, these living thermometers.

December 5

Venus is as bright as she will be now, resting high up
in the eastern horizon after sundown. These past few
evenings have been clear and dry, making her stand
out all the more.

It is an irony that she is so bright, made so that we see
the smallest fraction of her surface; her position to
Earth is close in our orbits, and because of this we see
her now as a crescent, reflecting much in the same
manner as the moon when it lies thusly juxtaposed.
Her closeness to us intensifies her light, and seen
through a modest telescope, she does indeed take the
crescent shape.

Her time as the evening star will fade, as she swings
through her orbit between us and the sun. She is
sinking slowly on the horizon each night and won't
reappear until five months hence as our morning star,
preceding the sunrise.

December 6

The weatherman forecasts icing in a couple of days as
a warm front with rain from the south gives way to a
fast moving arctic clipper, come down from the Great
Lakes.

We're nearly at the anniversary of the big ice storm
that happened a few years ago here in town; the
evidence of its damage is still visible. This is

particularly the case this time of year, when the absence of foliage makes the tree branches stand out well into the woods.

Throughout town, there are still "hangers" and "widow makers" from that past storm, branches that succumbed to the weight of the ice and snapped, yet remained fixed and dangling from the point of breakage. Of course, many fell to the ground long ago, and the majority snapped and fell during the storm itself, breaking power lines, damaging roofs and blocking the road. We recall how throughout the night of the big storm, large limbs were breaking several a minute, sounding like gunfire around the house and through the woods. The morning light revealed a landscape of icy beauty and sheer destruction.

The thought of another storm of ice coming, even if a minor thing, sets our nerves on edge.

December 7

During the last December ice storm, the majority of town went without power for a week, and the roads were nearly impassable for several days because of downed trees and limbs by the hundreds. The morning after, the building gray light revealed Grove Street as an almost unrecognizable stretch, everything covered in ice shards that glistened, save for the debris that continued to fall from the trees.

We were without power for eight days, living in our
fireplace room to be near the wood stove, using
candle light in the evenings to move about or to
simply pass the time, and we daily gathered water
from the Artesian spring in the woods near the
college. All the while the town worked throughout to
clear the roads of debris, using the field parking lot as
a staging area for placing the piles of limbs and full
trees, stacked well high of fifteen feet and the length
of a football field.

December 8

Ahead of the storm, a light snow fell overnight laying
just a dusting of white on the ground and in the
evergreen boughs.

Across the road, the sere brown of September's
pepper plants contrast well against he field of white.
Within hang shriveled fruits that were passed over
when the harvest took place, remaining on the plant
until the deep snows cover them until spring.

The color throughout is quite pretty, varied shades of
red, yellow and orange, hundreds of them within the
rows making a patchwork of white and brown with
splashes of color that look like ornaments on
miniature bare trees. Each pepper is but a diminished
version of its autumn form, resembling a lantern
mantle, dangling and infused with its own color,
defiantly resisting the encroachment of white which
will all too soon dominate the landscape.

December 9

The pelting sound began after midnight, lightly at first and hardly noticeable as light tapping sounds on the roof.

We looked out the front window to see the street light, expecting to view falling snow of some form captured by the amber glow cast downward from the pole. Rather, the screen outside the window was caked with a rain that had begun to change over to ice, giving the window a stained glass appearance of muddled orange light made diffused by its covering.

The pelting were the ice crystals, falling in earnest and combining with a misty rain, glazing everything in a sparkling wonder.

December 10

Yesterday's ice storm seemed to catch many people off guard, which is nonsensical really. It is December after all, and the fact we haven't experienced any significant snowfall yet is simply good fortune.

Several townsfolk are out today, wrapping their hollies and such bushes in burlap – something that should have been done a few weeks ago as an ounce of prevention. We are just as guilty as the next, and this small storm shamed us into our own last minute wrapping.

I both enjoy and dislike this chore, the former because the burlap has a pleasing odor all its own, like harvest and autumn somehow captured within. The latter is my own fault, as the procrastination then necessitates wrapping in cold temperatures.

The three big hollies by the front dooryard were wrapped in little time, and they will be moderately protected from the snow that drifts here three feet or more. Soon, it will be so deep that they will be buried altogether, awaiting their unveiling next spring when the thaws arrive, making us feel like archaeologists unwrapping the coverings of some unfortunate casualty.

Three winters ago was particularly bad, with heavy snows in town that came in mid-November and didn't let up. Unbeknownst to us a rabbit had become stranded beneath the burlap of one of the hollies and was fairly well buried for some time.

That spring, when the burlap was removed, there wasn't a single holly leaf to be found! The rabbit had stripped the plant to survive and had left a large pile of droppings underneath.

December 11

The male cardinal is perched atop the peak of the small shed near the stone wall that divides the berm from the access road. All around him, the light snow is falling gently straight downward, collecting steadily as a layer of powder on every surface, including the brilliant bird. He sits patiently watching the juncos, who are in a frenzy upon the ground beneath the tube feeder, which is empty from the morning's desperate activity. On occasion, he shakes lightly to rid the snow that has settled on his back and crest, making a flicker of striking red color against the backdrop of brown trunks and collecting white snow.

Without any wind, this snowfall is nearly idyllic, drifting downward in no real hurry, yet settling on the Earth measurably. The lower arbor vitae have shelves of white all throughout their boughs, weighing them slightly so that the each sags just a bit to the ground, opening the trees more fully until small avalanches occur. These trickle down, cascading and causing others to dislodge, making a powdery cloud of mixed snow that finally settles on the ground below.

December 12

Yesterday's peaceful snow is a reminder of the calm and beauty that often accompanies winter here. It allows us to accept the transition more gracefully, to acknowledge that the work and leisure of our autumn pursuits have indeed come to an end, and yet to see that there is still a landscape of beauty just beyond the window.

We are near the start of the long rest now, where the days of readiness and growth, production and harvest are all only memories of accomplishments. The gentle snow of yesterday is a newly lain blanket upon this

Paxton ground, coming like a welcome sigh to usher in this time before the cycle begins anew.

December 13

The birds have increased their presence at the side yard feeders, draining both tubes of black sunflower seed in just under two hours. There is a large storm to hit tomorrow, bringing a foot of snow that is to fall steadily through the day. The birds must be anticipating its arrival and are stocking ahead. We are no different really, as the grocery shelves will be empty of milk and bread by this afternoon.

A small downy is having difficulty with the pole, landing near the crook to get a closer look at the tube but not getting purchase on the metal still covered in a glaze of ice from the storm several days ago. He has only a moment at the top before sliding slowly down the pole, all the while gripping it with his diminutive claws.

At the bottom, he plops amid the seed-covered snowpack, looking nonplussed as best I could tell, before flapping quickly to the top once more. Again he descended. This went on for five rides, before he gave up and took to the lower woods.

December 14

A gibbous moon hung near the meridian late last evening in the calm and cold night that awaits the coming of the storm.

The thin covering of snow on the back porch crunched and even squeaked a little as I made my way across to a spot where the moon was visible up high between the boughs of two tall spruces that sit beside the access road.

There wasn't the slightest noise about, apart from my own breathing, which created small clouds of steam when backlit in the moonlight.

Off to the west, the starlight was blotted out by the approach of frontal clouds – the coming of the fury that is to blanket us with drifting snow.

A few wispy clouds passed just in front of the moon, moving quickly and very high above. For a brief moment, as the moon emerged in full from their veil, the clouds resembled trailing vapor against its disk like the tail of a comet which glows in the light.

December 15

The benefit of nor'easters is that they tend to depart as rapidly as they arrive; yesterday's tempest came in the late afternoon, with darkening gray skies that typify the oncoming of snow bands. By evening and then throughout the night, the snow fell hard, hitting the house and drifting all about. The wind fairly roared for several hours, as the low of the storm came and went, moving up the coast toward down east Maine.

We stayed snug in bed, listening to the howling wind and driving snow, knowing that by daybreak the landscape would be transformed and the work of digging out would begin. Apart from the storm sounds, there was only the periodic roar of the town plow making its slow path up Grove, its blinking yellow lights diffused in the falling snow and reflecting momentarily on the bedroom wall as it passed slowly by.

By morning, the wind had settled, and the clouds began to break, revealing a landscape blanketed in white 12 inches deep.

December 16

Two young boys walked by on Grove this afternoon, each pulling a sled behind him, trailing ten feet by a twine that stretched from gloved hand to runners. The road itself is still heavily snow covered, it being simply too cold for the salt to do much good, and the plows tend to neglect this section of town.

Thus the boys trudged slowly by, leaning forward in order to gain purchase in the drifts on the street, bound for the steep hill on the town soccer field.

Once we finish the driveway, I imagine we too might decide to go sledding there, for the hill is steep and drifted in, making for a short yet thrilling ride.

December 17

The thermometer read 1 degree this morning in the darkness well before sunrise. December's full Cold Moon sat twenty degrees above the horizon to the west, through by comparison to the moon of six months ago it is so noticeably farther southward.

It is tempting to consider most things by comparison, when it seems as though darkness and cold are gaining the upper hand. There is deep snow everywhere now, and we fear that we may not see the lawn again for months.

But beneath the drifts and within the frozen ground lies the dormant seeds of tomorrow's promise. We must have faith in this knowledge, that though the deep greens of summer's splendor have now long gone, its fruits lie waiting in this period of quiet.

So too we rest now, taking greater pleasures in the company of home and hearth, secure in our understanding that renewal comes only after slumber.

December 18

A calm snow last evening created a fluffy coating on
the upper side of every tree branch in the woods,
making them stand out as if highlighted.

In the morning daylight, little red made his way from
his winter nest in the barn to our dooryard feeders,
and I caught sight of him initially as he navigated the
aerial highways of criss-crossing branches. As he sped
along, seemingly unaffected by the powder of snow
along his way, bits would become dislodged in his
passing and fall gently as crystalline clouds to the
ground below.

All this was backlit by the rising sun through the
woods making the light refracted slightly within each
falling powder so that small rainbows were created
briefly within.

December 19

The town plow knocked over most of the reaching
brown stalks of the knotweed on Route 122, those that
just two months ago were yet green. The leaves had
since fallen away, leaving the drying stems bare and
searching, leaning across the guardrail on the north
side of the road and taking advantage of the small
shoulder there.

Now most of this is destroyed, made so by the rolling
wave of snow as it came off the angled plow blade,

arcing across the rail and hitting these plants with such force. They lie broken amid the slushy pile, down below in the wetland basin just off the shoulder.

By chance a small series of branches remained, and even more surprising is that their dried seed pods still clung to the brown limbs – small, 3 winged things, there were perhaps a dozen or so that fluttered gently in the breeze made each time a car came passing by.

December 20

A large buck deer moved furtively through the side north woods, having emerged from the field across the road, stepping quickly over Grove Street and into the berm that forms the small stand of forest that separates our house from the next.

I only knew of its presence, because I had glanced briefly out the front window in the fireplace room to see if snow was falling, revealed more easily in the amber street light out by the road. Just then the buck crossed, quickly into the trees and headed for the lower woods toward the wetland or toward Turkey Hill.

Two weeks ago, the woods were rather full of hunters, who would have relished the chance for such a sight. I suspect this buck has lain low since, only now more comfortable traversing its corridors, as the hunting season has begun to wane.

Winter

Rest

December 21

The ancients knew to celebrate this day, as do we, whether solemnly or with joy. We know that the darkness which has slowly consumed our passing days since summer, will now give way, retreating as our Earthly inclination toward the sun grows.

The solstice officially happened several minutes past noon, and on the verge it was tempting to think that for a moment we straddled two seasons, the autumn that just was and the winter that will be. Of course it isn't so defined we know, and this year in particular has seen December in cold and snow so that we have to remind ourselves that it is December and not January.

We look forward to this day, symbolically perhaps more than anything, as the long months of winter lie waiting just around the bend. Yet soon enough the rays will strengthen, slowly at first, almost desperately, warming the ground and the trees, melting the ice and snow, and assuredly shifting the season from one to the next.

Celebrating this point is our own accomplishment, one that will temper the harshness of what January and February will bring. We know that these seasons pass one to the next just as the solstices come and go, marking our progression and giving us hope.

December 22

A warm front roared in overnight, causing the temperatures to climb to near sixty degrees by morning, thirty degrees higher than anything we've experienced for over two weeks.

How strange that this first day of winter arrives like spring, with warming air over the snowpack causing fog so thick in the morning light. Large streams of water pour down the hills of Grove Street, in places as sheets of flowing melt water that establish ripples within.

December 23

By the end of the day, the steady rain and temperatures in the upper forties had all but erased the snow pack of the past several weeks. Throughout the day we watched as the lawn slowly reappeared, initially just the high spots peaking through as small verdant islands seen from our front window. Over the course of several hours, these islands expanded, as if the remaining white was a sea of water that was slowly draining away, until at last the land was revealed complete.

The knot garden too emerged, first the bricks of the border standing just above the snow, and in time the garden itself was laid bare. What a difference though from what we'll see in several months! Now, the Earth revealed is still lifeless as the autumn's sere remnants are all that sit within, apart from the scattering of oak leaves caught in the groupings. There are no yellow-green shoots of daffodils, or wanting bulbs of crocus or snow drops, no grasses or patches of white fungus from the warming soil.

This melting is an early thaw and nothing more.

December 24

The tractor was out this morning moving up and back along the rows across the street, pulling behind a large mower deck to cut down all the skeletal stems of last autumn's crops. With the snow gone yesterday and the return to the twenties today, the ground must be hard enough to accept its passage.

These past few days have been disorienting, firstly on account of the warmth and melt, and now to both hear and see the tractor in the fields. It is tempting to think that it is April, despite the return to cold.

In the afternoon we took the dogs around the perimeter of the field, letting them run ahead in the dirt of the two track while we walked slowly behind, looking across the rows that were mowed where now only stubble pokes through the soil. All about are shredded seed pods and stems, un-harvested crops and bits of weed.

December 25

We joined our friends across the road for Christmas dinner late this afternoon. Though the last of the harvest and sale ended nearly a month and a half ago, it still feels special to share time in the middle of the day, even if the farm is fallow.

In the warmer months, we become so used to seeing activity across the road from sunrise to well after sunset – such a hurried pace to accomplish work that never seems to end. Where summer was a rush to simply keep up, and autumn was busy in harvest, December is a time to merely rest, both in body and spirit.

December 26

A flock of brilliant cedar waxwings landed in the crab apple trees that front the college, nearly unnoticeable if they hadn't begun their high-pitched chirps. They feasted on the remaining berries still dangling like miniature darkened cherries in small clusters; the birds having no hesitation in moving quickly from one to the next.

They stayed for only a minute or so, unperturbed by my presence just beneath, until an unruly murder of three black crows came to inspect, landing on the white cross nearby and calling in protest. The cedars seemed to depart as one, making a last collective call before lifting off and flying up high toward the west.

The silence lasted only a few moments, till the crows became bored and looked for other victims to bully about. They too lifted one by one, noisily squawking for no apparent reason and flying toward the farm house to search for someone else to pester, I suspect.

December 27

The year closes in a few days, and we have known Paxton through beginnings and growth, maturity and harvest, decline and rest. It is tempting to think of endings now, as if the slow succession of these passing seasons has been experienced as such, as a linear passing of this thing we call time. We can't, as the ancient Greeks proclaimed, "step into the same river twice."

How wonderful to see it through to this point – not the end, though, as it is tempting to believe, but rather to know that the cycle of the seasons begins anew.

This is the real wonder – to know what is yet to come, that this river of experiences in this Paxton year returns upon itself; that we have stood not within the river, watching as the months and seasons have flowed past, but rather we have been carried along.

December 28

Not one to linger too long with Christmas decorations, we moved the tree from the sunroom to the outside. This has become a small tradition each year – to place the entire thing, still in the stand, propped beside the tube feeder just off the porch. Until spring arrives, we then enjoy an evergreen addition to the side yard.

The birds certainly seem to appreciate this, for within minutes of setting the tree in place, several chick-a-dees alighted on the boughs nearest the feeder, using them as cover I suspect from the potential of the red-tails or the falcons. They'd hop flight quickly to the tube, reach within to extract the seed, and return quickly to the Christmas tree to open the casing. The juncos too seem to enjoy the new addition, as do the mourning doves, both milling about beneath like chickens in a barnyard searching randomly for cast-off fare.

Meanwhile, the sunroom floor was littered with dropped needles from our moving the tree, and we collected these with a dustpan, enough to fill a half-gallon bag. I took these to the fireplace room, spread them quickly on the crackling wood in the stove, and watched as they sizzled and smoked, making the room fragrant with a tinged piney odor.

December 29

Fred had used the tractor to clear some of the sumac and briar from the lower ground next to the western fields, in an area that seeps moisture in even the most dry summer stretches. This acre has been fallow for several years, allowing these early colonizers to take hold and thrive, the briars notably so to the point that walking through has been nearly impossible.

Now there is access to the woods beyond, where the land dips into a valley formed by run off from the artesian spring. On still days, it is possible to hear the flow of the water from a hundred yards away, coming from within the folds of the small valley. On winter days, when the snow lies deep and the temperatures stay well below freezing, it is a curious sound to hear the running water.

It emerges from a six-inch pipe that rests within a rock shelf, clear water that flows neither forcefully nor feebly but steady, dropping roughly two feet into a small basin before making its way down slope toward Pine Hill Reservoir – a third of a mile through the deep woods.

On either side of the pipe edge, affixed to the lip in a mass and tumbling over and down six inches is a bright lime colored grouping of moss, striking now against the muted color of stone and brown leaves.

The water is crystal clear, cold, and wonderful to drink. It was a lifesaver for us five years ago this December, when the ice storm knocked out power for over a week.

December 30

The moon's cycle is nearly complete, for its new phase is due to arrive two days from now on the new year. The crescent this morning was merely a sliver of brilliant yellow, cast against the still dark southeastern horizon at just before six. In this shape, it is easy to see how tilted our own axis has become, as the moon's concavity points downward notably toward the sun, which will make its appearance in over ninety minutes yet.

I went to the middle of the town fields on Grove to get an unobstructed view of its rising and also to bid a silent farewell. Tomorrow's forecast is for flurries, arriving with a front coming through this evening; surely the clouds will cover the final sliver in the morning.

I stayed fifteen minutes, bundled just enough to keep away the morning cold and long enough to see the brightening of the eastern sky.

December 31

December is at an end as is this Paxton year.

It feels out of place to write about endings now, for the truth I've discovered is that one day, one month, one season does pass slowly into the next. There are no beginnings and endings really. There is only the steady succession of this cycle of the seasons, and if we are careful, we may get caught up in its beauty and its wonder.

January

January 1

Before dawn, bright Venus was just lifting on the eastern horizon through the bare trees of the lower woods. And if not to be outdone, Jupiter descended to the west, above the hills that border the farm field across the road.

Soon these two will depart from the early morning, Venus fading closer to the approaching sunrise as she recedes around her orbit. Her time as the morning star is ending for now, and we will miss her familiar presence of these past several months. We'll look for her again in the western sky as the evening star of spring, following the setting sun.

Jupiter continues to recede, made so by our own passage through the heavens as December has given way to January. Soon, it too will be absent from the dawn sky.

January 2

Along with a new year came a day of cold winter wind. The barometer is on the rise after the storm of two days ago, and we look forward to a stretch of cold January temperatures with blustery days and clear, still nights.

We are assaulted by a January wind unlike a summer breeze. I'm not referring to the temperature, of which the difference is obvious enough. The winter wind presses against with more force in a way that no comparable summer breeze can muster. The physicists will tell us that cold air, being more dense, has more molecules in a given volume, and so a twenty mile per hour winter breeze in every sense hits us with more punch. I believe them.

January 3

Astronomically, today is when the orbit of the Earth brings us in perihelion, or at the point closest to the sun. It is a matter of a million miles or thereabouts closer than at the furthest point, aphelion. The difference is really inconsequential against our average distance of 93 million miles.

Still, it's hard not to consider the irony for us folks in the upper portion of the Northern hemisphere, where we are in the early stages of another winter. Today in particular I don't feel closer to the sun, at least as far as the temperature is concerned. The thermometer read 0 degrees at 5 this morning, and a light breeze surely meant below zero wind chill.

But at least we are past the solstice, slowly and inexorably tilting back toward the sun. Soon its rising will start to creep backward in time, and we will look for it to shift more easterly through the trees in the lower forest.

January 4

I took the dogs for a walk this morning, cutting through the singular line of spruce pines that sit across the road like a fence and bordering the farm fields. These pines are surely mature by now, after having been planted as a break by the elder Cournoyer some 60 years ago.

As we passed underneath to the field, I looked up through the boughs, interlocked and swaying in the morning breeze. These trees shelter many different birds and squirrels throughout the year but particularly now when much of the ground cover and low bush is either covered in snow or bereft of leaves.

These same trees shelter us from the northwesterly gales that often blow in the winter. They break both the wind and the drifting snow as they come across the field toward the house.

These trees are well known by an acquaintance in town who works the power lines. Each year we lose one or two of these giant pines to the wind or ice, and they invariably fall to the leeward roadside, coming down on the power line or blocking the road. Last December, in a violent windstorm, the power went out on account of one of those trees crashing down. No sooner had my acquaintance come with a crew to cut the tree and restore the line then did fifteen minutes later another tree do the same.

Just across from the house, there is still a line of these trees, though as I pass between them for the field I wonder if they will all survive this winter's winds.

January 5

This morning I walked the dogs on the familiar field perimeter, starting again through the spruce line and into the edge of the farm field. From there, we typically walk slowly counter clock-wise around the farm using the two-track access roads that go from one field to the next.

The snow from a week ago is still nearly six inches deep, though quite fluffy, and it is amusing to watch the dogs undulate ahead of me through the drifts.

Nothing but a snow ridge distinguishes the separation of the two tracks where the farm truck drives, and here it is a bit more forgiving for walking. I know these roads through all seasons, and while the grasses between the tracks have their own vital appeal, there is still beauty to be found in the snow-covered paths.

On occasion, a sere golden rod or cluster of brown Queen Anne's Lace pokes through the snow, defiant of being knocked over. It seemed only yesterday that these were filled with the colors of late fall, but here they now stand as a brittle reminder of the season past.

About midway across the field, I found a singular golden rod husk bent over nearly horizontally and lightly touching the snow surface with its remnant flower heads. It was broken at the base so that the wind would cause the plant to shift around in a circle, and when I stood to look just so, I could only see a field of brilliant white powdery snow and the golden rod husk with a series of concentric circles it had made.

January 6

Our road is a dead-end street which passes by a small college and an area set aside for town recreation fields, on its way separating our house on the eastern side from the Cournoyer farm that borders on the west.

In the mornings when I am returning from some exercise, I like to walk the last hundred yards of the road to our driveway with my eyes skyward. This is particularly the case on the winter pre-dawn hours, when the skies are clear and the approaching dawn to the east is just beginning to occur.

The road bends slightly to the north at this point, and looking upward I easily spot Polaris at roughly 40 degrees altitude from the horizon. Grove Street forms a tunnel of trees here, with large spruces that line the west side and a mixture of oaks, maples and cherry on the east.

As the dawn nears, the sky on such mornings turns nearly an iridescent blue, what we call a Maxfield Parrish sky. Parrish painted dawns and twilights using layers of paint and varnish to create a unique effect. On certain winter mornings, Mother Nature does the same, and I admire the nearly black tree outlines on either side of the tunnel, with the Maxfield Parrish dawn and Polaris to bring me home.

January 7

We're in the start of a January thaw today, with temperatures in the upper 30s, brilliant skies and barely a breeze. Mostly because I wanted an excuse to go outside, and partly because I thought I should shovel the snow from the porch, I went out to the back yard just before noon.

There wasn't a whisper of breeze, and the midday sun was blissfully warm on my face, so much so that I just closed my eyes and tilted my head slightly back, like one of the Easter Island statues.

It was after a minute of this that I heard them down in the forest that borders our back yard. Unmistakable. Two Pileated Woodpeckers were calling to one another in their laughing sort of a trill. Pileateds are beautiful birds to behold, especially if you are fortunate to be close enough to watch them at work carving out a hole. With a striking red cap, black body and banded face, the contrasts of this large bird are simply beautiful. Unlike the smaller downy and hairy cousins, the Pileated tends to be a shy bird – which is why you more often hear them deep in the woods rather than see them near the house.

A rare treat for me. No sooner did I hear their calls then did they both fly in parallel over the house toward the field across the road. As distinctive is their call, their flight is equally recognizable as a series of rising flaps and falling rests, a mixture of flap-up, flap-up, rest down, flap-up, flap-up.

January 8

Today is a promise of what will assuredly come in a few months.

At midmorning, the temperature rose above freezing with the rising sun and calm winds. Our January thaw is temporary, we know, yet at its outset we can't help but feel rejuvenated thinking that winter will release its grip and spring will one day arrive.

My favorite part of the thaw are the earthy smells that carry on the breeze. Just last week, my winter walk on our access road into the woods was cold and snowy and in every way felt like January. The sun had seemingly little warmth, and there was none of the woodsy smells.

Today is almost a spring-like feel, and this same walk hints at life reawakening. There are the sounds of water dripping off the laden boughs of the evergreens, and what gentle breeze passes carries the familiar smells of leaf mold and soil and humid Earth. I walk in my footprints of last week, when the snow was nearly a foot deep, and now those places that I compressed with each step are nearly melted through, revealing the Earth and detritus of last fall.

We know that winter will return soon, cruelly in a way to remind us that the long haul is still ahead. But we are turning the corner on January soon, and the sun is ever so slowly getting higher in the sky. These brief glimpses of spring are our reminder and hope that cycles do come around, that nothing lasts forever, and with patience there is reward.

January 9

Not everything associated with the thaw is a welcome relief.

The sustained warmth and sun on our roads has caused frost heaves to occur. These are curious things to me, as we didn't have frost heaves where I was raised in the Midwest.

As I understand it, the warming temperatures during the day melts some of the frozen ground, including any within and beneath the road bed. Then, when the temperature drops below freezing at night, the water re-freezes, and as ice expands, the resultant pressure pushes upward and outward with such slow and yet incredible force that even roadbeds are buckled.

It is a commonality of New England, the frequent thawing and refreezing, especially during late winter, a costly nuisance to road maintenance where cracks and potholes form with time.

January 10

A few days ago I wrote of the promise of spring, and I am particularly thinking of this today. Inevitably and thankfully in the midst of the winter season, when we start to lose hope of ever seeing the grass again or the strident calls of the emergent insects or the return of songbirds to the dooryard, the seed catalogs arrive in the mail.

They have nearly the same effect upon us as do any exotic travel brochures. We browse from page to page looking at the beautiful images of fruits and vegetables in full ripeness or of wildflowers mundane to unique. Yes, there are familiars, like places we have frequented. And there are rarities within that we might like to try and plant, as an adventure to attempt when the season arrives.

Seldom do we purchase seeds from these catalogs (and it makes me wonder why they keep us on their list). Still, we enjoy them simply as a diversion through winter, an anticipation of what is to come, and a remembrance of seasons past.

January 11

Down the access road from our house, just after it takes a bend toward Asnebumskit Pond, there is a cluster of white birch trees set back roughly fifty feet into the woods. It is a grouping of six trees, with their individual trunks meeting commonly at the base and each trunk going off in its own direction. I've noticed that many birches form this arrangement, possibly having started as shoots from a mature three that felled long ago.

They are beautiful in winter, especially when the diffuse light of a gentle snow or even winter fog darkens the background just enough to contrast their whitened bark.

There really aren't that many birch trees around here, at least there aren't as many as I'm told existed in this area years ago. Ecologists claim that the birch prefers a colder and somewhat moister climate, and the global warming patterns of the past 20 years have shifted the growing niche of birch trees northward. It's too bad, for I enjoy seeing them in any season.

When I was young, spending summers in Northern Michigan, we used to make crafts out of the birch bark. Native Americans have long made use of birch trees, from using the bark as a covering for canoes, as a water container, and even as a food substitute. The Ottawa and Ojibwa tribes still carry on a decorative art of making small boxes out of birch bark, festooned with animal and flower designs on the surface made out of porcupine quills. My mother used to purchase these and keep them in our cottage, and I liked to open the boxes to smell them, for the Ojibwa would line the edges with dried sweet grass. It would smell like perfumed summer sunshine, and the smell lasts for years.

We would find a suitable white or even paper birch, one with a large trunk and pristine bark. Then we'd take a pocket knife and cut just a few layers into the bark, making a large square cut on the trunk about the size of a sheet of paper. We'd carefully take the edge of the knife to lift one of the corners away from the tree and slowly peel out the entire square whole.

It had the feel of thick cardstock. The inner side would be beautifully tinted in light and darker brown, matching the white and black patterns on the outside. On this inner side, we'd write poems or sayings or draw pictures. Then we'd light a match and slowly burn the edges of the square to give a burnished look.

January 12

Our son called down to us from his bedroom just before dinner, as the fading twilight made it still possible to see into the woods from his bedroom window. He had spotted a barred owl not 40 feet from his window, just inside the border woods on the north side of the house. The own was perched on a bare branch of the large white pine that dominates this portion of the woods. It was sitting still, occasionally turning its head to and fro, I suspect searching for its own dinner vole or even rabbit.

We hear the owls particularly this time of year, either in the early morning as they call to one another or in the evening twilight. The horned owl is the more familiar, with its comical "who who" call and repeated answer. I once had a conversation of sorts with a horned owl in the early predawn last fall. It started a call from far away in the lower woods, and I answered from the back porch. Back and forth we went for nearly five minutes, with the owl moving closer and closer every so often, as it tried to figure out what sort of relation I was. I have to admit that I took a little conceit that my call had garnered such an official curiosity.

The barred owl is another thing altogether. Its call has been described as a kind of "who cooks for you," and this does capture the essence. I've tried calling to the barred owls when I've heard them in the woods, but I suppose my dialect for barred isn't up to par.

From my son's window, we could see both the owl and a short distance through the woods the road that passes before our house. Just then, a person came walking up the road, and we watched the owl slowly and silently track the passerby with its head. The walker was unaware of this beautiful creature so close by, just as I suspect that the owl was unaware of our watching it from our window.

January 13

The thaw is to continue only for another day, then the weatherman tells us that winter will return in earnest. I checked my barometer this morning, and sure enough the high pressure which has dominated these past few days is giving way to a change.

This thaw has been a welcome relief.

Last night, the snow continued to melt on the roof, and I listened to the dripping sounds of water falling from the eaves, thinking that it sounded like an evening spring rain, gentle and soft as it falls drip, drip from the roof to be collected in the warming ground.

January 14

With the large cold front that arrived late yesterday, our January thaw came to an abrupt end. Really a part of me was relieved, for this thaw was strangely warm and lasted too long, though I admit to liking the early taste of spring. However, I was becoming concerned that the trees would start to respond in bud too early or that there would be an unusual insect hatch; it was that warm.

Often after the front passes in the winter, when the winds dissipate and the sky remains clear, the evening stars can be brilliant, particularly if the moon is closer to new. This evening was just so. Brilliant.

Orion rose just after 5:30 this evening, sitting sideways on the eastern horizon. I grabbed my small cassegrain telescope and sat on the back porch, where the familiar stars of his belt and sword came just into view over the top of the trees in the lower woods.

Just within the sword rests the great nebula, visible to the naked eye as a cloudy path among the resident starts. Though my modest telescope, the nebula takes up the field of view as a milky white and ethereal cloud, with numerous stars within.

I sat for a minute or so, letting my eyes adjust to the dark, looking at the nebula and allowing my mind to wander. The image looked winter-like, with shades of whites among the blackness of space and stars strewn throughout like snowfall collected on the pine boughs in the woods below.

January 15

I awakened this morning just after 4 am and out of habit went to make a small pot of coffee to help get things going. Also out of habit, I glanced out the window over the sink, first to look at the outside temperature (28 degrees) and then to see if the sky was clear.

Just on the western horizon lay Orion, although this morning it sat on his right side, slowly moving toward the treeline. In truth, only the two bright stars that form his shoulders, Betelgeuse and Bellatrix plus the trio of the belt stars were really visible, but even so the familiar pattern was recognizable.

Given my viewing last evening at 5:30 and this morning's at 4:00, I suppose the best time to view Orion in total would be midnight. The constellation would then be nearly at zenith, which is the optimal place for star gazing, as the light from the distant stars passes directly through the atmosphere. On horizon, the light is more filtered through the air, reflected and refracted ever so slightly that the twinkling is more pronounced. Midnight is best for Orion in January, but who wants to brave that hour in the cold?

January 16

I wrote before of the brilliance of the evening stars in the winter skies. Much depends on the cloud cover, of course, and it is the case that we so often have leadened skies in January, which cover the sun and the nightly stars.

This makes the clear nights all the more spectacular, when the stars seem as twinkling pinpoints against the dark of space. These stars seem closer in winter as if we could sweep our hand across the sky to gather them together.

Summer skies lack this character, as the evenings are more often laced with humid air that carries the scents of verdant growth. It is this very air that gives us such wonderful sunsets and twilights that linger on. But this gives way to starry skies that are seen through a humid sheen, however so slight, that the stars look more filtered and dream like.

Though the summer nights fulfill the senses in their own way, for me the skies of January fill us with an austere clarity, of contrasts of light and dark, cold and warm, life and beyond.

January 17

We keep a birdfeeder just outside the sliding door of the sunroom, set on the end of a shepherd's pole that is driven into the grass. Each morning my wife Sarah fills the tube full of black sunflower oil seeds and puts any excess in a little pile on the edge of the porch.

After weeks of this daily practice, the area around the feeder is littered with the cast offs that birds pull out of the feeder and drop on the ground below. It gives the snow a deeply peppered look.

I am watching around the feeder today, only because we have this jittery red squirrel whose antics around the porch are irresistibly comical. The red squirrel is one of among several resident squirrels that consist of roughly five ground and our singular red. We also have flying squirrels that live among the trees, but as they are largely nocturnal, we rarely see them and only occasionally hear their calls.

Our red typifies the petulant manner that Beatrix Potter so aptly describes in several of her children's stories. He darts about defiantly often stopping to posture with two legs pushed forward and head held upright, chittering his warning call and briskly flicking about his tail.

Defiance will just as quickly give way to retreat when a passing shadow or sudden noise startles this mercurial little thing.

He is a hoarder that one, like all such rodents, and I suspect that the easy pickings of the sunflower cast-offs provide a ready supply of energy. This is particularly true as I believe the red may have forgotten more buried caches than he can remember, and what's to worry when food is provided?

January 18

I mentioned flying squirrels, and we've experienced these first hand. Since moving to our wooded home, we suspected that flying squirrels were about when we began to notice their high-pitched shrill of a call in the summer and fall nights. A year or so went by without any sightings, until one late fall day I received a phone call from Sarah in the middle of the day. She had a close encounter with one of the shy little troublemakers.

Evidently, one had slipped down the chimney pot that feeds into our beehive oven next to the big Rumford fireplace. Sarah heard the racket of something scurrying around in the fireplace room. When she opened the door to investigate, there was the flying squirrel, clinging desperately to one of the curtains next to the window. It evidently had the good sense to try to escape.

Sarah opened another one of the windows in the room, grabbed a long handled broom and placed it gingerly next to (beneath) the squirrel, whereupon that little creature transferred its grasp to the bristles. After moving the broom slowly to the open window, the squirrel made a quick leap into the void and glided away down to the woods not 20 feet from the house.

The only other encounter happened just this fall, and I've never seen anything like it before. We were out in the front yard finishing up raking the last of the oak hold outs when all of a sudden I saw this object fall from one of our tall maples that sits next to the garage.

One of our terriers (Tag) saw it drop to the ground. He rushed over and reached it first, and my only glimpse as I approached confirmed that he bit into some creature that was momentarily stunned after the fall. Tag was reluctant to let go, and I can only imagine what was going through the dog's mind about squirrels just dropping from the sky like manna from heaven.

The squirrel lay dead on the ground, and I grabbed a stick to help transfer it to the woods. Flying squirrels really are beautiful to see; the distinct separation of brown fur on its back from its whitened under belly, with its large skin fold between its legs and large darkened eyes. It is unmistakably cousin to the grounds and reds but adapted to its own way of life that makes it a curious and beautiful thing.

January 19

A light snow happened last night, putting down just under 4 inches and making everything around look cleaner and more winter like. With the morning sun shining through the lower forest trunks, the back woods took on the look of an Ansel Adams photograph, all contrasts of light and dark, straight lines of branches set against one another in snow.

We walked the access road at midday, silently creating our own path through the snow, crossing over tracks from various creatures that had trafficked there through the night. This is the real wonder of new fallen snow. It reveals the passage of what normally goes unseen, often no more than a stone throw from your own dooryard.

We recognized rabbit tracks, squirrel, several deer, and something that looked like a large cat's print. We've only seen the bobcat once, last fall as it basked in the lower garden sun early in the morning. It stayed long enough to hunt a few birds to no success then furtively padded away. The tracks today are possibly from this same cat.

January 20

Warmer today, near 45 degrees, with a frost-driven wind all day. The snow is melting quickly in the brilliant sun, and now the tracks we saw yesterday stand in relief. It is a curious thing, those tracks of the animals and of us are the last things to completely melt, which then leaves the compressed snow of the track impressions plain to see against the revealed detritus of last fall's leaf litter and Earth.

The wind spells change, and the front is bringing arctic air tomorrow. January is living up to its namesake – Janus, two faced it has been this year more than I can recall in the past. Back and forth we've gone from thaw to freeze.

January 21

The cold has brought the Junco's out in a frenzy to the feeder. I am fond of these winter birds, for they remind me of a well-dressed diner, who is content to browse on the ground for his fare.

The juncos are a harbinger of winter, normally arriving in late November as they leave their summer breeding sites up in the mountains of New Hampshire and Vermont to settle for the winter in our neck of the woods, among other places.

They frequent the feeder area, usually in larger groups, and are fairly sociable birds, though not quite as gregarious as the chick-a-dees. They tend to hop and scratch more than chick-a-dees will, trying to dislodge seeds below the snow or soil. When startled, the juncos are clear warning signs of an intruder, like a passing falcon or red-tailed hawk. As if in unison the Juncos scatter in all directions, quickly vanishing to the underbrush or forest to escape a threat. I suppose the markings that so nicely camouflage them in the summer are a liability in the snow cover, as the darkened tops are more easily distinguished against the snow.

January 22

A morning for winter empiricism like no other. Let me explain. I am overly sensitive to this subject, sometimes to the point of righteousness which in the end probably doesn't accomplish what I intend.

It was bitterly cold this morning, somewhere near 0 degrees with a light breeze out of the Northwest across the field and toward the house. I bundled up to take a walk around the Cournoyer fields at 5:00, well before even a glimmer of dawn.

I may have looked a little silly, bundled up in several coats, a hat, facemask and such, all to ward off the bitter wind chill.

The walk was fine enough, with freshly fallen snow crunching faintly beneath my feet, but the experience reminded me of what it must be like to be an astronaut on a spacewalk. I couldn't feel the wind on any part of my body. My hearing was nearly blocked from all the layers, with the exception of my breath which when exhaled in the masks and earmuffs made a noise like a scuba air hose.

Aside from my motion (and what I could barely glimpse through squinting eyes), there was really no connection to the walk. My experience was separate from the sights, sounds and feelings that so normally are a part of being "in" the moment – the empirical nature that is the essence and beauty of simply being outside.

I watch my own students on campus, and in so many ways their own behaviors embody this empirical disconnect. They, like so many, spend more time living and communicating virtually with devices and one another that they have forsaken the genuine importance and worth of experiencing, of feeling and being an active participant in their surroundings.

Winter is a time for such battles, with the harshness of a morning walk filling my head. There's nothing better to crystallize this point than to remove the coverings, of which I did. Boy, it was cold and felt of winter, so austere.

January 23

Today is a perfect example of yesterday's empiricism. This morning was just below zero, again with a light breeze that made the wind chill certainly bitter. There was also a gentle snowfall, with strangely large flakes that I normally associate with wetter snows.

Standing just outside my garage, I watched the snow drift downward and occasionally settle on my dark jacket, each flake so large that it was easy to distinguish the individual patterns. Under more temperate mornings, those flakes are ephemeral, with enough residual heat on the jacket to melt the patterns before they can be clearly seen.

I stood for a while and looked as closely as I could. Truly beautiful things up close, and they do seem to be unique to one another, built on a general rule of having six sides. Some were greatly branched and intricate beyond imagination, while others were so simplistic they reminded me of the child's craft of folding paper and using scissors to create a simple flake. I couldn't resist using my breath to watch them fade away, the solid molecules picking up enough energy to liquefy – the outer points first giving way, followed by the center hubs.

It is overwhelming to look at the snow pack in our yard, now just at seven inches deep or thereabouts. All those snowflakes, one upon another, pattern after pattern, seemingly endless forms of creation that serve no purpose of which I am aware. Eventually, they will all yield to the coming warmth, returning to the ground or to the air.

January 24

A loud crack within the house sometime in the middle of the night awakened me, and it took a few moments to realize what it was. Bitter cold had caused something in the house frame to shift enough to give off such a loud snap. I got up to look at the thermometer on the kitchen window, and it registered -5 degrees outside, and I could tell that a moderate breeze also blew.

I hadn't heard the house crack like that since before we moved here – our old farm house in Kalamazoo would creak and pop in the bitter cold. In truth, I don't think we've had such cold temperatures in years, and I suppose it may be on account of the global warming patterns. To read the accounts of New England winters from decades ago makes you realize that weather temperatures have moderated in the winters. Writers frequently recount bitter stretches of days and deepening snow, where the tendency to sit by the fire and hunker down waiting for a break. We contract in winter, look inward, and conserve our own spirit as well as our bodily heat. The cold outside forces us inward, waiting and hoping. Perhaps this is what our house is simply doing.

January 25

I saw a robin today in the bare branches of our lone apple tree in the front yard. It regarded me for a moment with its dark eye, ringed with a small white band then took flight toward the spruce line across the road.

I so desperately want to think of it as a harbinger of an early spring, but I know that some robins actually do overwinter in our area. What they consume, I can only guess. Perhaps some of the winter berries which still cling to the shrubs. Those robins that I do occasionally see in winter are quiet, where in spring they will erupt each morning in birdsong.

January 26

The angle of the noon day sun is just perceptibly higher in the sky than it was a month ago For the first two weeks of January, I kept fooling myself into believing that this were so, but now I do think it to be true.

It is a minor victory as we've turned the corner from the solstice, marching ever onward in our seasonal shift.

It is more apparent in the coming of the dawn and setting of the sun; our days are lengthening. Still, this doesn't mean we can start putting away our winter clothes for lighter wear. It is still cold out, after all, and thought the sun's rays strike more directly and for longer with each passing day, they are yet oblique enough to generate much warmth. Any that we do receive must arrive with a coming front, normally on the heels of an incoming snowstorm that blossoms from the southern Atlantic states and works its way to New England.

Patience though. Soon the sun's rays will penetrate deeply enough within the ground and trees, awakening the pulse of life within. Soon enough the frost and ice, glistening now in the noon sun, will yield to the warmth, retreating cold giving way to the vitality of another spring.

January 27

January Wolf Moon

This night feels like one in which wolves may come silently across the fields, pausing only to gaze skyward and cry out. We have no wolves here, but coyotes visit us from time to time, and their strident calls in the dead of night are as familiar and similar to those of their lupine cousins.

We particularly hear the coyotes in the early fall, when the nights are just starting to cool enough, yet our windows may still be open to let in the evening fresh air. On these nights, the sounds of the waning crickets and evening flying squirrels are the usual chorus, which is a pleasant background for falling asleep. This makes it all the more jolting to be interrupted by the eerie barks and pitched calls of the coyote packs, ranging somewhere in the fields across the road.

Tonight is a night suited for wolf calls, like some beast made living in a Jack London story, sitting on the knoll in the Cournoyer field and howling upward to the clear moon.

January 28

I took an old glass rolling pin, which is hollow inside and sealed with a screw cap top, put charcoal chips down in one end, and filled it roughly with 1/3 full of good soil. To hold it, I crafted a stand out of wood, designed so that it held either end allowing the central tube of glass and soil to stand upright, with the screw top located at the top of the roller, so that I could open it periodically to water within.

Into this terrarium I sprinkled several tiny seeds from the Sweet William Catchfly that grows wild near our knot garden out front. I had collected the seeds last fall, placing them in a small labeled vial and on an old typeset shelf hanging on the wall where 30 to 40 other such vials reside with collected seeds of differing wildflowers.

It is a small accomplishment really, and the chances of the seeds germinating within in the relatively cool temperatures of our January house may be low. We do such things at this time of year precisely to build our hope that life and growth will soon begin anew. These hopes we nurture just as I will do with this terrarium; that with the right amount of light and warmth and luck and timing we may be fortunate to witness another beginning in the cycle of the seasons.

January 29

After a week of temperatures in the teens, a warm front came in last night, brought on by a steady wind and light rain. With the snow cover still trapping the resilient cold of the week prior, the humid air turned as foggy as I've seen it here, to the point that the mailbox at the end of the driveway was lost in the mist.

A fog like this in winter is strangely out of place, particularly as the driveway remained glazed from the mist that froze in contact with the still cold pavement.

January 30

Deep in the woods early this morning, a fox was calling a warning cry. It was a strange and unsettling sound – a series of clipped barks and earnest cries that signaled some sort of danger.

We haven't seen the foxes around here since the fall. I was beginning to think that the frequent vixen from late summer had moved on or worse come to some unfortunate end. We enjoyed watching her throughout last summer, coming and going in search of food to bring her litter of three that sheltered beneath an out building down the road at Robinson's Greenhouse. She became quite tame in a way, not minding if we stopped to watch her trot by through the woods.

I had begun to think that she had moved on this fall, after the kits were grown enough to be on their own. This morning was a bit of a shock, really. The fog from yesterday still lingered, and the waning gibbous moon filtered through enough to give the landscape a twilight look, though the trees of the lower woods were hidden through the mists. I stepped out on the deck to feel the air and to listen to the water dripping off the roof (which is always a pleasure in January). Apart from a gentle southern breeze that stirred the trees and moved the wind chime, it was fairly quiet.

The cries came out of nowhere, from far off in the lower woods. It was startling to the point that it really did make the hair on the back of my head stand up, as the saying goes. I can only imagine what would cause such distress. Perhaps a fisher cat or coyote was on the hunt. The cry was so unnerving that I decided in no way was I to investigate.

Only one other time and also in winter, can I recall such a visceral cry. Something must have attacked a rabbit near our house, and the cry of what must have been its death throes were simply frightening to hear.

January 31

January at an end. I know that I should accept and even anticipate each day, even those in the midst of our New England winters. Still, I admit that I am usually pleased when January has come and gone.

Seasonally, the weatherman indicates that winter begins in December and lasts through February. I like this framework, even if I know it doesn't really apply. This would mean that we are two thirds finished with winter, and February's relative shortness makes it seem as if spring is possible, if only around the corner.

According to the celestial calendar, March 21st or thereabouts is the equinox, and the unofficial acknowledgement of our vernal return. This means winter is really just a month old at this point, following the solstice, and I for one find this disheartening.

No, winter holds tightly here, regardless of meteorological or astronomical calculations. It will also hold fast despite what the perennial prognosticator indicates in two days. I am resolved to ride it out and take a page from experience. It will be winter until it stops being winter, no sooner.

February

February 1

The moon was particularly brilliant this morning, following yesterday's cleansing rain and passing low. The skies actually cleared last night allowing the gibbous moon to peek through the thinning clouds as it rose on the eastern horizon.

Early this morning I caught the last glimpse of Jupiter just before it dropped below tree line, with the moon to follow in an hour or so. That the moon reflects so incandescently is a wonder. To look at samples of the lunar rocks and dust that were retrieved during the Apollo missions would cause anyone to doubt that we should be able to see the moon at all. For evidently, the moon is largely made from dark grays of various shades, yet even still the collective reflection from what looks like asphalt is enough for us to see a gleaming whitish surface with darkened seas and mountains within.

Scientists have calculated that the moon reflects 8% of the sunlight it receives and that such light takes only under 2 seconds to travel from the moon to our eyes. Seen against the backdrop of a winter morning, this 8% is enough yet to cast a shadow of objects, and I particularly enjoy a morning hike lit partially by moonlight. This diffuse light is enough to see my field trail, where sere golden rod and Queen Anne's Lace cast shadows onto the remaining snow, and my dogs are visible as whitish shapes up ahead, bobbing up and down.

February 2

As luck would have it, the thaw of several days ago melted all the snow in the backyard, clearing the grass between the door to the cellar and down the hill to the barn. In most winters, this stretch can hold 12 to 16 inches of snow easily until April, as it is partially hidden from the warming rays of any sunshine by the large evergreens that line the access road down to the lower woods.

Normally about now we run low on wood that I stacked in the cellar in two high rows (nearly a face cord). Cellar wood is warm wood, making it conservative of the heat when brought upstairs to the fireplace room. (Anyone who burns wood in a stove for heat soon learns that wood just brought in from the cold outside takes all the heat of combustion merely to warm the wood). In most years, this means trudging through the snow with a wood carrier, opening the barn door, navigating the incline into the dry barn, and ferrying one load after another up the hill and into the cellar. Today, however, was a small treat, as the ground was snow free and frozen hard from morning temperatures in the teens. This made for easy trips with the wheelbarrow, taking half the time and certainly half the effort. We have a full load in the cellar again.

PS: I discovered where our little feisty red squirrel lives. It was startled when I first entered the barn, nearly falling on my head from its nest in the eaves above as it scurried helter skelter to escape.

February 3

We had a dusting of snow last night, and this
morning was clear and cold with just the faintest
breeze. In the darkness of my morning walk, the
moonlight from the quarter moon was shining just
enough on the pavement for me to see the shifting
tendrils of drifting snow on the road.

It was beautiful, walking with the wind at my back
and the snow moving about in swirling patterns at
my feet. It reminded me of water spray on the lake,
when the wind blows fiercely and the tops of
whitecaps are sheared apart and sent tumbling from
one crest to another. The patterns in the waves are
just as the snow, shifting shapes of spray and foam
like a living thing that moves slowly across the lake.

February 4

The chick-a-dees seem to be in a frenzy this afternoon
at the feeder outside the sunroom. Sarah will fill the
tube in the morning with black oil sunflower, and by

midafternoon it is nearly ¾ empty. Spend time watching the feeder for a few minutes, and it is easy to see why the feed drops so quickly.

With four perching holes at the feeder, each has a chick-a-dee client almost continually. It is comical to watch, with chick-a-dees-in-waiting either perched on the top of the tube itself or the shepherd's pole or fluttering nearby waiting for a space to vacate. At one time I counted 16 birds near the feeder, all in a frenzy trying to get their fill of seed.

This degree of earnest foraging may suggest the beginning stage of preparing for the summer migration. Such birds will accumulate fat reserves from which they draw upon when making their long return flights to the north.

Without the feeder here, the birds would rely on the natural seed, cast off from either tree or weed, and likely they would forage in the lower woods or the line of spruce across the road. And in those non-mast years, when the trees produce far less seed, the birds are more earnest about their pickings. This may explain why it seems particularly frenetic at our feeder, as if the available food source in the surrounding woods is thin, while our high-protein sunflower is gluttonously plenty.

We'll enjoy them for awhile – the friendly little chick-a-dees, who seem unperturbed by our coming and goings, cocking their heads and regarding us with small beady black eyes as we pass closely by. They, the juncos and the titmice are our predominant winter small birds in the dooryard. We have our house finches, yellows, starlings and grackles, cardinals and jays. But the chick-a-dees remain our affable feeder tenants.

February 5

Another snow dusting happened overnight which put a fresh blanket of at most ¼ inch on the ground. And, just like a couple of days ago, the snow was nearly weightless and fluffy – the kind in which you could simply blow gently on it to move it about.

This snow is water poor, meaning that the frozen crystals of water are large, where pockets of air can easily reside within. It is a snow made for shuffling through, where no moisture seems to accumulate on your pants or shoes. It is not a snow for packing or shaping, for the fun of snowmen or snowballs. This is the snow we often see in the artificial globes, turned over and again to make the white particles swirl and dance as if carried effortlessly on an imaginary eddy.

More often than not, here in Paxton we receive the dense, water-laden snows borne by nor'easters that collect humid air from the south before falling from the sky upon us. This is the heavy snow of winter and while enjoyable to shape and pack, it is nevertheless a burden to the shovel and to our roofs.

Light snows are ephemeral things, dancing in the wind and alighting on the ground. They vanish quickly with a moderate sunlight. I like these snow globe storms that come and go.

February 6

Thinking more of snow today. The weatherman predicts a major nor'easter in two days hence, and evidently we are to receive between 12 to 20 inches of heavy, wet snow.

This means work of the physical kind, and so much snow at once makes it difficult to enjoy it much afterward.

Years ago in college, I took a course with the comely title of the "Physics of Snow" as a part of my general studies. (I thought wrongly at the time that the course would largely address aspects of snow skiing). What did interest me the most concerned the characteristics of avalanches – how they are affected by the weight, crystal structure, age and incline of the snow mass, among other variables. If we do receive a heavy snow in a couple of days, I will think about these variables when I watch the accumulation on the roof. This is particularly true for the valleys of the joining roofs, where drifting and settling can cause pileups of 2 feet or more.

February 7

The sun was brilliant this afternoon, still angled enough to stream into the sunroom, blocked only by the branches of the woods that border the access road. It is really only at this time of year that direct sun enters the room, for the spring leaf in the trees and the rising sun in the vernal sky make direct light impossible.

It is easy to forget how closed in the house becomes, when the forest reawakens with vibrancy and the spreading leaves shrink our vistas. Now, I can look down toward Asnebumskit Pond and just barely see the sunlight reflecting off of its icy surface, visible between the trunks and branches of oaks, maples and ash that lay dormant.

The world seems bigger now, and our eyes can more easily look beyond to discover what lies out there. This is a welcome exchange in winter, which on account of the cold and dark we tend to draw within and hibernate. Better yet to see through the dormant woods, to the ridgeline far in the distance, to go there and further, if only in our mind.

February 8

A light snow began midmorning, gentle flakes that drifted in on an easterly breeze. This direction is unusual and ominous of what is to come later. Our winter winds typically situate from the north or northwest, following fronts that descend from the Great Lakes as Alberta Clippers.

Not so today. This storm had been forecasted several days ago as a mighty nor'easter which would bring possibly historic blizzard conditions over the day or so.

I started noting the barometer each hour today, recording with trepidation the readings: 30.2 at 8am; 30.17 at 9am; 30.15 at 10am; 30.05 at 12:00pm; 29.95 at 2pm; 29.92 at 3pm; 29.8 at 5pm; 29.2 at 8pm. The snow and wind intensified by 5pm, with nearly 3 inches of fresh cover and the trees across the road swaying dangerously. We sat in the fireplace room, with woodstove going full out to heat the room. Aside from the crackle of the wood and creaking of the stove, the only sound to be heard was the relentless wind against the house, truly a freight train noise blowing snow in all directions and making the light from the lamppost out front a shadowy figure.

February 9

The snow was still coming in earnest this morning, and while the wind continued to shape drifts outside, I noted that the barometer had started to rise slightly overnight. The nor'easter must be moving off shore of Boston, evident in the wind shifting to the north and pressure on the rise.

The door to the porch from the sunroom was nearly impassable, with snow having drifted in to the midpoint. Snow is abundant, having fallen steadily throughout the night as a light fluffy blanket made living in the swirling gales which created false mountains and eddies. The wind is a seeming living thing, picking up spindrifts of snow and sending them across the yard, around the barn edge and fleeing to the lower gardens.

The news reported 30 inches of snow here, with drifts to four feet in places, still accumulating steadily at midday, though periodic breaks appeared in the fast-moving cloud cover. We watched it move and shift across the front yard all day, leaving small patches of bare grass in the lee side of trees.

There's no sense in digging out just yet. We'll have to clear the driveway when the wind abates, otherwise the snow will simply drift in again.

By late afternoon, I noticed a tractor moving in the driveway of Cournoyers. Sure enough, the wind let up enough to make plowing a sensible project.

February 10

The access road that leads to the lower woods and Asnebumskit Pond is drifted in nearly three feet deep. This morning, I put on a pair of snowshoes and gaiters and trudged my way down the road toward the pond.

The snow remains nearly weightless and though deep it is fairly easy to shuffle along, leaving a series of small trenches in my wake. Sometimes, when the snow is like this, I'll bring the dogs along, and they follow behind my footsteps, using the trenches as paths to navigate the deep snow, porpoising from one patch to the next.

The winds from yesterday had finally lessened, and the cut in the woods that is the road leading to the pond is incredibly beautiful, with the morning sun angling through the forest and reflecting off of snow that covers nearly everything.

It is all the more magical to simply listen to the sounds all around – the barest whisper of a gentle breeze that flutters the sere leaves, the curious call of a chick-a-dee that comes to visit from a nearby pine bough, and the damping sound of snow falling from branches in clumps to the ground, set loose by the warming of the morning sun.

Compared to the fury of the past two days, when winter pinned us within the house and hearth, the gentle still of this sun-dappled section of the lower woods is revitalizing.

February 11

At the near edge of Asnebumskit Pond, just after the access road ends in a gate as the land berms upward toward the man-made dam, is a large section of Phragmites grass. This grouping is along approximately 50 feet of shoreline, with the reed stems situated just inside the shore.

They are easy to spot approaching the pond from the road, as grass heads reach nearly 15 feet into the air all swaying together like summer corn stalks caught in a breeze. The heads are sere brown, having dropped their prodigious seed last fall, yet resilient in lasting until the new cycle.

It's no mistake that the grass has successfully taken here, since the prevailing winds blow the wave action to this berm shoreline, where aberrant seeds can more easily colonize in abundance of sunshine and water.

The pond is an expanse of the purest white from the big snows of two days ago, and the Phragmites are cast in a sharp relief of brown on white with intermittent blue sky peeking through the heads as they sway back and forth. Come spring, when seed and shoot go to new plant and the emergent grasses begin to grow anew, the Phragmites gets lost amid the explosion of greens and yellows that populate this pond.

February 12

A sure sign of February greeted me abruptly this morning on my walk. Just down Grove Street, past the bend in the road near Robinson's, is a small trail that leads into the woods. The trail is a semi-maintained access point to the upper woods that separate Asnebumskit Pond from its twin Streeter Pond, which lies a quarter mile downhill. The trail crosses over a small creek that serves as the distributing watercourse from the upper Asnebumskit to the lower Streeter.

As I passed by the trailhead, the odor was unmistakable. A skunk had sprayed somewhat recently, and from the strength of the air my guess is that the offender might have a den near the culvert that affords passage for the stream.

February is just about right for skunks to become more active, usually intent on beginning the mating season. I am aware of this fact each year, but still in the midst of cold and dark, snow and ice, when the weather still cries loudly of winter hibernation it is a surprise to have such a familiar smell at a time when outdoor smells are all but absent.

Skunks really are curious and downright cute little creatures, and we have our fair share of them within a radius of our house. They are distinct in coloring too, and just when I become accustomed to the predominant black with diminutive white stripe, I'll come upon a largely white skunk. I don't suppose there is any selective advantage in color variants, though perhaps the Darwinian may claim the favorable nature of white in winter, though this is nullified of course in the temperate months. Perhaps variation is neutral, like the stripes of the wooly bears we see ambling along in the fall.

February 13

Thinking about the stream that leads from Asnebumskit to Streeter Pond. This time of year is favorable to hike the lower woods, provided that the snow isn't too deep. It is relatively easy to pick out the deer trails in the woods, with the lack of ground

cover and obscuring tree leaf, plus the poison ivy that
is a ubiquitous menace is at bay.

Follow the stream to Streeter Pond, and skirt the
shoreline to the opposite side, where Grove Street
elbows into Pond Street. Here, another stream outlet
drops more insistently as the landscape falls into a
miniature valley that descends toward Pine Hill
Reservoir. Roughly 100 feet from Streeter Pond, the
creek veers away slightly to the northwest, and there
is the remnant of a trail alongside. Though I doubt
that this trail receives more than a handful of curious
hikers in the span of several years, if you follow it
along for roughly 1/10 mile into the woods, there is
evidence of a time when this area must have been
quite active with human industry.

It took me a moment to realize what I was seeing,
when I came upon a fairly large pit that was situated
between where the trail had veered away from the
stream and the water, which was flowing more
quickly on account of a fairly modest drop in
elevation. The pit was filled with about a foot of
snow, perhaps less in those areas were the filtered
sun could reach. The give away was the stone lining
in the side walls, partially obscured by years of in
growth from the surrounding vegetation. I suspected
that this was at one time a foundation, and its location
next to the stream strongly hinted at a potential mill.

Sure enough, just near the stream, not 25 yards away
from the old foundation, was an unmistakable
millstone, roughly 30 inches in diameter, sitting
amongst other debris of the forest. The stone was

badly covered in lichen and moss, and heaven knows how long it has sat there. What a curious find, seemingly so far from the center of our town, yet an important vestige of its settlement past. A 1961 booklet I obtained from the town's Historical Society indicates that the old Pine Hill Farm operated no less than three mills on this creek site somewhere between 1755 and 1830.

February 14

On the far side of the farm fields, in the woods below what is called the lower field, is a small, dilapidated square outbuilding, nearly 4 foot on each side, with the vestiges of a hip-style roof. In the summer months, it is impossible to see this building, because the overgrowth of vegetation blocks any view into the woods. As it is, even in the winter when the trees are bare and the ground vegetation of golden rod, sumac, tall grass, and various ivy is largely gone, the outbuilding is still difficult to locate among the trunks and branches.

Actually, it is easier to find by sound, if the wind is light enough so as not to mask the noise. Just next to the building is an artesian spring, which runs all year, even in the bitter cold of January and February. The building may have at one time been a small storage shed for collecting water, or perhaps an abandoned pump house of some sort.

This spring lets forth a continual stream of the most crystal clear, clean and notably cold fresh water. For our family, this spring was a lifesaver a few years ago, during a notable December ice storm that disrupted power in Paxton for over eight days.

Because I knew of the spring, each day I would trudge through the snow across Cournoyer's fields, carrying two five-gallon buckets to fill. The tree fall in the woods near the spring on account of the ice damage made access a little tricky, but through careful stepping and ducking I was able to reach the flow.

I'd fill both buckets and bring them back to the house, one for water and the other for washing dishes or for use to flush the toilette. It was rustic living these eight days, where darkness came early, and we huddled close to the woodstove reading by candlelight with tea made from the water of the artesian well steadily brewing on the stovetop.

February 15

A small south facing patch of snow next to the moon garden looks as if someone has sprinkled pepper upon it. The springtails have emerged as if on cue to the warming sun and retreating snow.

There are myriads of them, jumping about so slightly that it is difficult to notice from several feet away. Yet up close, they are a frenzy of activity as each tiny springtail explodes forth, moving no more than a fraction of an inch on the snow surface.

Yesterday, I didn't notice their arrival, though the conditions were decidedly less warm and the cloud cover predominant. Sometime today, they emerged from adjacent ground, exposed by the warmth, to jump outward onto the snow.

They are small harbingers of our coming spring, these small insects that serve to forage the detritus of last year's leaf litter. They are known as *Collembola*, but the familiar name more aptly describes their curious behavior.

February 16

By midday, under clear skies, the sun had warmed the air temperature into the upper 40s, and with only a hint of a breeze it felt warm out. It is a relative warm, of course. I think about this notion, when the sultry days of summer stretch one hazy day into the next. I play the game, thinking of coming cooler weather, imagining it to be 50 degrees, if only for an instant – to break the hold of the summer swelter.

40s for an afternoon in summer would feel like ice against our bodies, whereas today under the sunny skies it is a delight. No need to pretend of moments of summer warmth to ease the cold stretch. Nature has released her grip, if only for a day or so.

The snow melts in earnest, and even the dormant grass is showing in spots that didn't drift too deeply from the storm of last week. Small rivulets of melt water create little rivers on the driveway, pooling into small puddles in the low spots near the grass edge. There they will endure, until evaporation, for though it is indeed warm, the ground remains frozen just below. Water must wait to seep into the Earth.

February 17

Mr. and Mrs. Cardinal have been visiting more regularly, coming tentatively to the tube feeder in the morning and again just before dinner. He is the more timid, preferring to sit cautiously in the branches of the small spruce that borders the access road. He watches her descend to the snowy ground beneath the feeder, as she hops gingerly, cocking her head about to select those sunflower seeds that have been cast aside from above.

He is strikingly red now, in almost sharp relief within the dark greens of the pine, peppered also with dusty snow to give it all a mixture of greens and whites with a singular splash of cardinal red.

February 18

Our transient pack of juvenile delinquents has returned to the feeder area. They come just after first light, bounding in from the direction of the lower woods, I suspect coming from their elevated nests that we can see in the tops of some of the larger hardwoods.

At anytime, there are roughly four or five of these gray squirrels around the porch, eating as much of the cast off seeds as they can find, while also inventing new techniques of raiding the feeder itself. They are a comedy to watch, occasionally alternating between solitary feeding to interacting with one another as they play and quarrel around the dooryard.

When they arrive, our little red squirrel tends to leave, for it is apparent that their niches don't overlap in harmony. To listen to little red, one would think that he rules the roost, with his incessant chattering and stamping of his feet announcing and protesting the arrival of the pack of grays. No sooner do they invade then does little red scurry, sometimes across the snow in the back headed for his nest in the barn, while other times up the big maple that dominates just beyond the feeder. The grays settle in, one after another to eat and play and scold among themselves, while little red runs along the highway of branches, chattering away in protest.

February 19

The air returned to a frigid breeze all day, blowing steadily and hard from the northwest. Though the sky was a crystal blue, and the sun came directly enough to provide some warmth, the winds conspired to keep the chill in the mid 20s even at midday.

A light snow must have happened overnight, and the steady wind was enough to drift the new snow across the fields, through the spruce line and spill onto the roadway. I took the dogs for an afternoon walk into the fields, though the footing was more precarious than I had anticipated.

The snowpack of perhaps 6" deep had formed a crust on the first inch or so, covered then just slightly by the light snow that drifted throughout. To step in our familiar trail was an adventure of step, hesitate, and wait to see if a boot would break through the crust to the downy snow beneath. The dogs had more success - their light weight staying secure on the crust as they moved quickly through patches of more heavily drifted areas.

February 20

Over the snowpack that encircles the big sugar maple which dominates just beyond the bird feeders in back, a small vole came scurrying just so. It skirted the base of the tree, using the bare grass on the leeward side as cover, pausing just enough so that for a split second it blended in. Then, for reasons I can only guess it darted around the tree and disappeared from view.

We tend to see the voles more often this time of year, as warming temperatures and more insistent sunshine work on the snowpack. As it recedes, small tunnels begin to appear, which reveal a complex network of passages across the side yard. Actually, it is the snow above the tunnels that melts, and with the tunnel floors having been compressed by frequent use, the effect is that slight lines of visible ground become revealed when the temperatures rise.

It is tempting to think that activity ceases in the ground and below, as creatures either perish upon the first frost or resort to hibernation or torpor, shut away in some ground nest or den. Where these highways of tunnels lead, I can only guess, but I can report that there is a general confluence around the cast off seed that peppers the snowpack around the feeders. So we have both trespassers above ground coming to get their fill with gray and red squirrels, rabbits, and the infrequent raccoon. And, we are invaded in secret from below.

February 21

The vernal pool is draining again, now that the midday temperature is warm enough to melt the small spillway that crosses the access road. Just a few days ago, this little stream was frozen through, stopping the outward flow of the pool uphill. Now, though there is a skin of ice on the surface, the flow of water is visible just beneath, interrupted only so with small pockets of air or bits of last autumn's detritus made loose by the slowly receding pond.

Come late spring, this flow will cease altogether, isolating the wetland and its budding fecundity. The water is mostly clear now, though soon it will be laden with a myriad of life from algal growth, phytoplankton, zooplankton and the awakening hordes of amphibians and invertebrates which revive this marvelous ecosystem.

It will be from here that our hylas will begin to call, signaling the awakening of life and the beginning of another vernal cycle.

February 22

Our little red skittered among the maple branches at midday, under a warming sun that took the temperature near 40, following a night in the teens. His movements were at first peculiar, seeming to jump forward only a few inches at a time with his mouth touching the branch here and there.

Upon closer look through the binoculars, it was evident what I had suspected; little red was testing various points of the branches for wound sites, where building sap had begun to ease out in tiny amounts. And so little red would lick, move on, lick, and continue.

The timing is on schedule, and a reminder of our slow change in season. The warming day after such a cold night has created sufficient pressure difference in the maple, and what we anticipate in early spring, maple sugaring season will soon be upon us.

The sugar farmers won't begin tapping just yet. No, we need more days of warm and nights of cold. Perhaps a week or two out, and then we'll begin to see the taps and buckets hanging about the trees, put there by those still inclined to reap the maple's bounty. For now, we enjoy the early harvesters, the squirrels and birds who also take in this special treat.

February 23

On the knoll that fronts the entry field to Anna Maria College, I stopped to watch a small group of Cedar Wax Wings flitting among the small copse of crab apple trees that sit alone at the summit. The now sere fruit still dangles in profusion from the bare branches, small apples that are no more than ¼" in diameter and slightly shriveled. No matter, for the birds devoured them readily, with reckless gluttony.

They seemed completely at ease with my standing just under the branches of one of the trees, while they hopped about putting apples into their mouths in astonishing succession. Striking birds that remind me of masked bandits, similar in a way that chick-a-dees do. With their curious nature though, chick-a-dees resemblance is overshadowed by their friendly demeanor. The wax wings are aloof enough to better assume the bandit persona.

And suddenly as one, the small flock rose quickly into the air and was gone.

February 24

The light of the nearly full moon shone brightly enough to illuminate the feeder area in the porch dooryard. Just before turning in to bed, as is the habit I called the dogs to go outside for their nightly bathroom, and I thankfully caught sight of it in the moonlight just before I opened the door.

Sitting unaware underneath the feeder was a small opossum, digging intently at the snowpack to locate hidden seed casts. It was healthy looking as far as I could tell, though opossums aren't exactly the model creature of aesthetic.

Just then, one of the dogs, Tag, barked a series of terrier yelps, and the opossum waddled quickly into the small berm that separates the dooryard from the access road. We watched it cross the road, easily lit by the overhead moon, enter the woods to the south, and make for the neighbor's barn.

February 25

Today is the full moon, know as the snow moon, and it has lived up to its namesake. We received 6" of heavy wet snow throughout the day, sticking well to the pine boughs and arbor vitae, bending them over in protest.

I feel the same way this time of year, as February is about to give way and we begin to chomp at the bit for signs of the season's change. These late winter snows, so often laden with moisture, weigh heavily on the body and mind. We can take comfort that the snows of late February and March may come in like an unwelcome lion, but the days warm too insistently now for them to last long. We begin to see patches of dormant grass here and there in the sunny spots, and certain buds of pussy willows and magnolias are unmistakably swelling.

So come visit, old snow moon, and know that tomorrow you will begin to wane.

February 26

The pine boughs, bent over from the burden of the heavy snows of yesterday, spent the day slowly releasing clumps here and there as the temperatures rose. It was late winter's own version of the symphony we look forward to hearing in spring, when the rains drop incessantly from the budding trees and roof eaves, making rhythmic notes. We anticipate these things after the long winter, which apart from the wind and sleet, is bereft of common sounds.

It is a small awakening of sound, of course, but it is a harbinger of the chorus that soon awaits. If you listen carefully, it has begun in the creaking of the road bed that heaves with frost and thaw. It is in the slow movement of the sap in the maples, rising in earnest to fuel the budding of new growth. It is the robin's song or the titmouse's call, which has changed ever so slightly in signal of the coming spring. Soon we will leave behind the cold sounds of winter winds against the house or the still, soundless nights of January where no noise interrupts the silence in the woods.

February 27

As if sharing the anticipation, a young pair of red-wing black birds were at the feeder today. At first glance, it was difficult to identify them, save for the fact they were of something different than our usual titmice, juncos, chick-a-dees and finches that predominate during the daytime in winter.

Only the smallest hint of the red portion of the epaulet flashed as the birds foraged on the ground below the feeder. Still, we can't help but smile, knowing that within the next month we will hear the nesting call of these males - prrriiii deeee, prrriiii deeee, as they await the coming of the females.

Those shoulders that conceal will then proudly display the red and yellow, a badge of masculinity to attract a potential mate.

It snowed briefly this afternoon, followed by a driving sleet. February gives up slowly, and I wonder if the black birds experience regret.

February 28

February at an end. It is a time of transition, even if it comes as an ebb and flow. It is easier now to reflect that winter has gone by quickly, when we are nearing the end, and spring fever is beginning to settle in. Late November seems like a long time ago, when we steeled ourselves for the coming darkness.

The winter has its own vitality, though in a different sense. As the nights grow longer and cold descends, we turn to our own fires both physically in the hearth and spiritually in the mind. It is a time of reflection and of search for meanings, when brilliant night skies display infinite possibilities of places so remote. We can't help but search for our place and purpose amid all the contrasts of beyond and within.

March

March 1

It is surely early spring when the great horned owls earnestly have their morning conversations. They must have awakened me at 3 am, and I lay in bed for an hour listening to them calling back and forth.

One must have been just next to the house, on the north side in the small copse of woods. On occasion we will spot an owl, either great horned or barred, perched in the mid boughs of the large white pine that dominates just there. The other sounded farther away, perhaps deep in the lower woods where the access road bends toward Asnebumskit Pond.

They had quite a periodic rhythm, with one calling a distinct "hoo, hoo," followed by a pause of ten seconds or so. Then, the partner would repeat, followed by an interval of nearly a minute. This went on for over an hour, and I began to wonder why their conversation had reached such an impasse that they wouldn't change the subject.

Great horned owls can be easily fooled into returning a call. I've gone outside at such an hour, stood on the porch and called "hoo, hoo" to the woods below. Often this time of year I will receive a reply. Once I even coaxed an owl to approach from the woods, calling then moving, calling then moving closer. It must have stopped at the woods edge at the lower part of the garden beyond the barn. It called once more and was gone.

March 2

March is the unofficial beginning of frost heave season here in Paxton. Our own road has stared to buckle noticeably along a crack in the bed that runs down the middle, beginning just after the farm driveway and extending down intermittently to our front.

The town roads are littered with these temporal ridges and potholes, as the warming days and yet still cold nights expand and contract the moisture beneath. Our car rides like an old jalopy, bouncing along as if on leaf springs whose time has long passed.

This expansion of the soil is a powerful force, and we wonder at the way it shapes the landscape. The farm field is evidence of this enough, as the first crop of newly surfaced rocks should be ready within the month. Some are the size of an oak barrel, having moved ever so slowly year after year through freeze and thaw until it wormed its way to the surface ready for harvest.

Soon we will hear the tractors in the field, going slowly with bucket low to the ground so that one of the men can collect them. Another sign of spring.

One large boulder had made its way to the surface of the middle of the field used last year for cabbages. I suspect that when Fred was cultivating one of the tines caught alarmingly on the rock, which precipitated his using the tractor to fully extract it. There it sat for the remainder of the fall, propped upright in between the rows of plastic that marked the beds of cabbage.

I can look out the front window and see the rock through the spruce line. Though the field is sill roughly 8" deep in snow, the boulder sits nearly 2 feet up above the surface.

Yesterday, I took the dogs for a walk though the field, just in the early morning when the cold temperatures had hardened the snowpack enough so that we could walk on top without breaking through. The dogs were particularly interested in exploring around the boulder, for it is evident that our resident deer use the rock as a marker of sorts to locate the cast off cabbage that resides below the snowpack.

Leading up to the boulder from the far fields is a trail of deer tracks. They form a jumble around the rock, evidently where the deer had stopped to hoof at the snow in search of old cabbage, some of which has been now exposed to the air. The dogs obviously enjoy the odors, both of last year's decomposing cabbage and of the remnant passing of the deer.

For our part, when the sun warms just enough, we are patently aware of the decomposition. Old cabbage may be intriguing to the dogs, but I assure you that being downwind from this patch has its disadvantages.

March 3

I walked the field loop again this morning, despite the strong breeze with a wind chill to remind me that we may still have a long haul yet toward any definitive spring. As if to emphasize this point, a light coating of snow must have fallen last night giving the landscape a clean, winter-like appearance.

The footing was good around the perimeter of the field, and the snowfall revealed several tracks that must have been made at some point during the past 12 hours or so. Here was the spot where a rabbit had come across the stone wall that borders the north part of the field. Its indecision was written plainly on the snow, as it evidently stopped, circled several times, and retreated hastily to the stone wall.

Further down were field mice tracks, perfectly preserved in the snow dust as tiny impressions in a line, weaving ever so slightly across the field expanse. I followed them for roughly 100 yards, until an area where drifting had occurred had obliterated their path.

At the western stone wall deer tracks alongside what appeared to be a following dog, perhaps fresh on the scent and trailing the deer. The dog's paw was large, and I wondered what stray was patrolling these fields in the pre-dawn hours.

More surprising was the tractor tread patterns that met me near the corner of the southwestern wall. Of course, I stopped to consider if it likely that either of the men had driven down this way so early. Were it the beginning of the summer, I wouldn't need to question this, as the tractors are usually out each day in the hour just before dawn. Today, with it being 7 am and just after sunrise, there was no reason to account for the tractor this far down the field.

The tracks were fairly compressed, extending in a relatively straight line up the snow-hidden two track that leads from the barns. I followed them toward the barn, trying to figure out any rhyme or reason, and in the end had no conclusions to make. The tractor tracks were a mystery to me, just as so many of the small critter prints in the snow.

March 4

The old maple up the road had little ice sickles
dangling from a few places where small twigs and
branches had broken away since last fall. This is a
sure sign that maple sugaring will begin in earnest for
those few who still hang the buckets from the maples.

It was cold enough this morning that the running sap,
rising through root pressure upward to the branches,
leaded out of these small break points in the maple
and froze into miniature stalactites of attenuated
sugar water.

Behaving just as the squirrels, I broke off a small
sickle to lick it, and sure enough I could taste the
faintest hint of sweetness.

Just west and south of Paxton in the Brookfields is a
large maple sugaring farm. We went to tour there a
couple of years ago, when the sap was in full
pressure. What an operation, with hundreds of yards
(miles?) of clear plastic tubing overhead, connecting
all the tapped sugar maples to a central collecting vat.
It was amazing to stand below one of the lines and
watch the semi-clear liquid flowing toward the sugar
house, a stream of sugar water interrupted
occasionally with tiny bubbles in the tube.

The sugar house was a small barn that contained a
large boiler vat of sorts, fed continually by a
voracious wood fire burning beneath. Evidently,
during the sugaring season, the fires burn night and
day for a couple of weeks on end, boiling down the

sap in the vats until the water component is
sufficiently distilled to leave the concentrated syrup
behind.

Like so many things, there was so much labor and
time for such a small yet sweet reward.

March 5

I heard it for the first time this morning, down near
the spillway on the far side of Asnebumskit Pond.
Somewhere in the sere stand of *Phragmites* a red-
winged blackbird sang its unmistakable "prrr deeee."
I could only stand still and smile, listening to this sure
harbinger of the coming spring.

It must be an optimistic bird, for the pond is still
frozen over, and the surrounding berm and
woodland is yet covered with at least 6" of snow. Yet
there it perched within, hidden inside the tall fronds
grasping a single stalk, swaying gently in the
morning breeze.

I stayed several minutes just to listen; the bird called
and paused perhaps a dozen times, and I couldn't
help but wonder the purpose of its call. The females
aren't due to arrive for nearly a month, so my sense is
that this bird might simply be proclaiming this
territory to would-be male rivals.

March 6

Drive along the roadways, or walk the back woods and you will notice the willows starting to yellow. If the light is just right, they even seem to create their own glow. The red and swamp maples are also starting to color in the stems.

Down on route 122 out of town, in the low area that forms a wetland which connects directly to the small lake inside Moore State Park, the road passes over a large culvert that provides passage for the wetland. On either side, but particularly on the eastern portion, swamp maples predominate around the low land.

They are starting to awaken so noticeably now, as if someone has painted on the stems a bare reddish sheen.

March 7

Given the recent uptick in bird activity, I thought it best to inspect the bird boxes we placed in the periphery around the feeder yard. All told, we have two wren houses and a large traditionally shaped bird house that has been home to chick-a-dees the past several years.

This has become a spring ritual, to open each of the boxes and clean out the nesting material of last year's occupants. Admittedly, I always feel a bit ashamed at doing this, because I suspect (and hope) that the soon-to-be arriving tenets will be one and the same from last year. I feel guilty in so easily removing the engineering concoctions of twigs, moss and grass knowing that the same birds will likely spend hours rebuilding.

The two wren boxes had typical wren nests –overly packed and notably large for such a small little bird. The chick-a-dee house gave me a start just as I began backing out the screws that held on the wooden base. The screws made a screeching sound on account of friction with the wood, and this caused the entire box to resonate with a high pitch as I turned the screw.

After a few moments of this, I paused because the box itself was making a deep vibrating sound within, and for the life of me I couldn't explain it. The vibration stopped. I started on the screw again, and no sooner did the vibration begin in earnest.

At this point, a child-like fear took hold of me, as I began to invent all sorts of irrational bird-box demons which were waiting to attack the moment the floor dislodged. Curiosity eventually overruled, though I admit to jumping back quickly as the last retaining screw released its grip and the floor dropped to the ground.

Wouldn't you know, in the midst of all the nesting material of grass and twigs and bits of dryer fluff – a queen bumblebee had made her overwinter nest. She drunkenly buzzed about just within the nest ball, awakened rudely from her hibernation.

March 7 b

The veracity of the groundhog is at stake today. Put another way, we've taken two steps backward in our seasonal progression.

In summer, I greatly admire Paxton's situation at high altitude here among the Wachusett Mountain foothills. When the lower towns just 8 miles from here swelter in the July heat and humidity, we often are 5 to 10 degrees cooler, which makes such a difference.

In March, it can be a cruelty, as early spring (or late winter, depending on your point of view) storms back in from the ocean. Just 8 miles from here it is raining, while Paxton is blessed with 6" of snow – a heavy, wet snow that sticks to the evergreens and sags them over.

I am looking out the office window now, watching the snow pile up in the raised garden beds down at the lower end of the yard. This same scene was a Currier and Ives picture in December, but my patience has worn thin in want of sunshine and the verdant smell of Earth. March is fickle, and the weatherman has forecasted a stretch of 50s in a few days.

March 8

It snowed all night and several hours into today, with a driving wind out of the east that is typical of a nor'easter low that sits off the cape. I took a ruler out to the back, in a spot that isn't subject to drifting too badly. Nineteen inches of new snow since yesterday afternoon and at least 6" more is forecast.

The drifts in our front dooryard are nearly four feet deep in spots, and the front entryway is completely blocked.

Just before bed last night, we checked the back porch to see if our surrogate new pet opossum had visited. She's been regularly coming now for the past two weeks, foraging under the feeders for discarded sunflower seeds. Sure enough, she was sitting right on the porch, using her front paws and long snout to push aside the snow that accumulated around her, oblivious to our watching her from only a couple of feet away.

Where she goes during the day is only a guess, but we've seen tracks that seem to lead across the access road to the neighbor's garden shed. And, when we first discovered her, the dogs gave chase while she ambled in that direction. (I kept hoping that she'd perform the coma-like seizure and drop dead, only to see what the dogs might do.) If she comes again tomorrow, JD wants to name her Pat.

March 9

The storm of the past two days is now gone, and the skies shine clear, though the wind remains fierce.

Sitting in the sunroom watching the birds return to the feeders in earnest, the wind must be out of just the right direction, as the hurricane chime in the front keeps sounding.

It's a fairly large triangular chime, that I fastened to the corner of the front barn. It's weight is heavy enough so that only a fairly strong breeze out of the north will cause it to sound.

It is a deep and pleasing metallic chime, reminding me of the sound of the harbor channel markers that sit off Woods Hole in the Vineyard Sound. The intermittent "clang, clang" I am hearing just now is oddly out of place amidst the snowpack and winter scene. In my mind, I see seagulls hovering just above the boat, and warm water wind blowing spray from the tops of the crests, sounding the big red channel buoy as it pitches in the swells.

March 10

As I walked past the town fields this morning just after sunrise amid nearly perfect stillness, I heard the slow "whoosh whoosh" sound before I spotted it.

Coming in low and traveling east from the direction of Anna Maria, a long blue heron flew overhead heading toward somewhere unknown.

For just a moment, as I looked upward so that only sky and trees and the passing heron were in my vision, I could easily imagine some Jurassic scene, and the lone witness to this prehistoric bird silently, save for the "woosh" of its wings flying by.

The heron evokes this sense of ancient creature, with its habit of flight and occasional guttural squawk suggesting some pterodactyl in hunt.

I see the herons now and again in summer, usually wading near the sore of the pond, silently and patiently hunting for some small fish or errant crawfish. They are elegant in water, albeit somewhat unsettling, as they cautiously walk the shoreline, stepping with slow and deliberate intent, all the while looking with their penetrating gaze.

March 11

It is warm enough today for me to sit outside on the porch, out of the wind and where my chair sits in the full sun. It is a glorious day, and it is reviving to feel the sunshine on my face and to listen to the birdsong.

I sit maybe 20 feet from our feeder, and after several minutes of my being here, the chick-a-dees show no hesitation at coming and going. The nuthatch is decidedly curious, remaining just beyond in the break line of the trees between the feeder and the access road. Less gregarious than the chick-a-dee, the nuthatch makes a slight humming call, not so much a social call, but rather a singular pip, I think inquiring of me and my purpose here.

The snow continues to melt off the roof in earnest, and the chorus of chirps and dripping sounds and the warmth of the sun against my skin make the storm of days ago seem in the past.

March 12

I have seen forty seven Marches come and go. Those of my childhood are distant to me now, and my memories are sketchy at best. The months and seasons and years have stacked one on top of the other, and I am acutely aware today of such timelines or yardsticks in which we measure our lives.

While standing in the driveway this afternoon, simply listening to the birdsong and enjoying the full strength of the March sun on my face, I was surprised to see a small midge-like insect flit closely by my face. It was carried along in a gentle breeze, likely having come from the direction of the barn and headed westerly where the breeze seemed to take it.

The first insect of the year, not counting the emergent ladybugs we often get when the sunlight warms their hibernation space in a windowsill crack. No, this was an honest-to-goodness flitty bug, as we call them. An ephemeral, I suppose, meaning that today it will likely experience the entirety of its life, having emerged today from a chance egg, lain last fall on a twig that awaited just the right amount of warming sunshine. Within today, this creature will emerge, grow, fly, attempt to find a mate, and ultimately die upon this Earth. No seasons or years that stack one after another. Just today.

As a boy growing up summers in Northern Michigan, we used to see the mayflies emerge upon the lake, often en masse, spending just a singular day or so in their adult winged form. I remember then, as I do now, how fragile life seems, how inconsequential, when the scales of time are but a blink to us.

March 13

A comet was supposedly visible for those of us in the northern hemisphere. According to the astronomers, we were to look low on the horizon just after sunset, and for a brief window of time, the comet would appear as a whitish streak in the twilight sky just near the point where the sun had set.

Seeing the horizon anywhere in Paxton is difficult enough, on account of the many hills and trees that encompass them. We planned ahead to drive to the top of Davis Hill Road, just ½ mile or so north of town, where I am certain that there is an unobstructed view to the southwestern horizon.

The sun was due to set at 6:30pm, so we started getting ready to go just about a quarter after 6, when Sarah noticed the large and dense bank of clouds moving in over the western sky.

After two days of crystal clear skies, both day and night, it seems out comet date will need to wait until it next returns.

March 14

Thinking more of cycles and seasons and timelines today, perhaps because we are in the midst of a change here from the winter that was to the spring that will be. The flitty bug that marked the change in one sense two days ago is long gone by now. Its short cycle is marked only within the day or two in which it lives. The comet is leaving our area, outward I suppose on its long journey to the reaches of the solar system, whereupon it will cycle its return Earthward again. I won't be here when it arrives next, many years from now, lifetimes for me, but just a blink in the eye in the cosmic sense.

Our lives are measured by cycles, days that turn into months, seasons that become years. Spring affords us a sense of beginnings and of possibilities, where we see the progression of cycles on so many scales, played out in the span of days and weeks. Yesterday's insect has gone to egg, maybe hatching anew in due time, and the spring comet will return again many springs from now.

March 15

Despite that the yard is still mostly covered with snow, there is a small patch on the western side in the front of the house that receives more sunlight throughout the day. Here the snow has given way, and we can just distinguish the matted Vinca minor within the patch, not four or five feet in diameter.

At the edge of the Vinca, just poking up maybe an inch at most are two daffodil meristem heads, pale yellow and snow weary, waiting for sunshine and warmth to spur them on ever upward and greener.

These are the first floral promises I've seen this year, and I am rejoicing inwardly. As the snow recedes, particularly around the knot garden in front, we may see the first tender shoots of crocuses and snowdrops soon.

March 16

After sunset last evening, we went to a high knoll on the north side of Anna Maria's campus, just south of a break line of cherry trees that marks the edge of the farm. From here, it was possible to see the western horizon without being obstructed by tree line.

The waxing crescent was just a sliver, like the Cheshire Cat perhaps 15 degrees above the horizon, set in a twilight zone that went from pink below to deepening blue-black as the sky ascended. As we often get in the winter months, when the sky is free of clouds, it was crystal clear with no humidity.

We had hoped to catch a glimpse of the fading comet, supposedly just 10 degrees to the west of the crescent moon, though we were warned that it had receded far enough from Earth's view to make it faint. So we waited and waited, scanning the sky with field glasses trying to discern the wispy tail set against the deepening black sky.

In the end, no such luck, yet the sky itself was resplendent with stars that seemed to awaken by the thousands. Jupiter shown brightly nearly overhead, and as we stood and watched the heavens, the bird song and breeze of the evening were around us.

March 17

The killdeers have returned. We actually heard one last evening while hunting for the comet. Among the chorus of evening sounds, a modest prelude to what we will hear in a month or so after sunset, a lone killdeer trilled its insistent tee tee tee tee, over by the lower field that is still covered in snow.

I think of the killdeer as a comical bird of summer, walking briskly on two spindly legs among the raised beds of the planted fields, staying just ahead of the tractor or walker. It is a mystery why they prefer the open fields as nesting sites, where all manner of dangers are a possibility.

I imagine it is the males that have arrived, with the females soon to follow, waiting for the weather to warm and the fields to be turned so that they can commence in building their exposed rocky nest.

We will hear and see much more of them as the spring ensues.

March 18

The forsythia is yellowing noticeably now, and it stands apart from the other shrubs that line the edge rows of the fields. A month ago, you wouldn't give it much notice, but now it seems to glow with expectancy.

We have a large bush on the northeast corner of the house that has a will of its own, growing wild in all directions and with a virulence of a summer weed. Each fall, I cut it back with a vengeance, knowing full well that by next mid summer it will be reaching upward in all directions.

Sarah took a pair of garden pruners out today and cut a few clippings to bring inside. Set them in a vase on the windowsill and wait a couple of weeks and we will have an early taste of spring, golden yellow flowers that precede the coming of the green.

March 19

March winds are decidedly different than just two months ago. They are at once more gentle and yet strangely biting if the day is just so. The cold winds of January were thick with air, packed closely together so that each gust was an assault. Now, the air is tinged with a coming warmth, where the Aeolus breezes are less forceful, and we feel less need to lean into the wind figurative and literally.

These winds carry a humidity from places west and south, and though they blow with less apparent force, we are stung nonetheless by a fierce chill. This is all the more as March winds seem more constant, as if the gods were apt to stir the pot to shift from winter to spring.

Today is such a day, where the wind built quickly in the morning sun and blew steadily all day, coming down the sides of Wachusett Mountain, across the snow-laden fields, and to our doorstep.

It is not the March winds of my youth, all filled with images of flying kites and early spring flowers. This may be the case in the Midwest, but here we seem locked in the transition between winter and spring.

March 20

Evidence suggests that the ancients did not revere the equinox as they did the solstices of December and June. Admittedly, it is difficult to celebrate it much this year, beyond a simple acknowledgement that tomorrow the days will be ever so slightly longer than the nights.

It should be a time to appreciate our balance sheet, which has accumulated a surplus of evening darkness since last autumn, at the expense of our precious daylight. Tomorrow, as the Earth begins to incline gradually and increasingly toward directness with the sun's rays, we should at least for a moment stop to savor this accomplishment.

I am telling myself this today, because it is snowing like a fury, which is an odd contrast to the weatherman's proclamation that spring has officially begun. Amidst the stinging snow, I decided to go for a walk down Grove Street, following the hill downward to the bend in the road just past Robinson's Greenhouse. At midday, not a soul was out on the road. It had the look and feel of a January day. Just 50 yards or so past the greenhouse, set within the woods on the west side of the road, a singular white pine stood out tall and straight against the backdrop of its deciduous neighbors.

I noticed this tree only because a lone cardinal was perched at it summit, calling its song over and over in what I could only characterize as jubilation. No matter the snow or wind or cold temperatures, "rejoice" seemed to call out this bird. Spring is upon us.

Paxton Wildflower Listing

Below are the approximate months/dates for seeing the blooms of these flowers. Of course this will vary depending on local conditions.

March

28	Skunk Cabbage
31	Crocus; Snowdrops

April

14	Coltsfoot
20	Grape Hyacinth; Daffodils
24	Vinca minor (Periwinkle)
28	Fiddlehead (various ferns)

May

3	Wild Strawberry
4	Trillium
5	Dogtooth Violet; Early Saxifrage
10	Bluets
12	Lilly of the Valley; Viburnum
14	Starflower; Shepherd's Purse
16	Lunaria Annua (Money plant); Robin's Plantain; Dandelion
17	Common Cinquefoil; Common Buttercups
18	Canada Mayflower
20	False Solomon's Zeal; Garlic Mustard

24	Wild Geranium; Mints
29	Honeysuckle

June

1	Chickweed; Wild Columbine
2	Sweet William Catchfly
3	Spiderwort; King Devil
5	Yarrow; Birds Foot Trefoil
6	Blue-eyed Grass; Nightshade
7	Pink Phlox
9	Wild Rose; Lavender
11	Orange Hawkweed
13	Daisy Fleabane
15	Milkweed
17	Greater Celandine
19	Virginia Creeper
26	Chicoree
28	Tall Meadow Rue; Wild Toadflax Smart Weed (Lady's Thumb); Swamp Candles (Yellow Loosestrife); Common Mullein; Black-eyed Susan; Sweet Peas; Day Lily; Coreopsis
29	Sundrops; Evening Primrose

July

2	Rabbit's Foot Clover
3	Queen Anne's Lace; St. John's Wort
7	Creeping Dog's Bane
8	Yellow Goat's Beard; Swamp Milkweed; Cattail
9	Purple Coneflower

| 10 | Wild Bergamot; Bee Balm |
| 14 | Teasels |

July (continued)

15	Joe-Pye Weed
16	Meadowsweet
17	Goldenrod (early sighting)
20	Staghorn Sumac
22	Soapwort (Bouncing Bet)
23	Yellow Tansy
24	Pokeweed; Jewelweed (Touch-Me-Not)
25	Rose of Sharon

August

2	Cardinal Flower; Pickerel Weed
20	Thin White-Toothed Aster
21	Indian Pipe
22	Knotweed
24	Ragweed
25	Fireweed
28	Boneset

September

| 3 | New England Aster |